Babies' Names &
EMBROIDERY

Cecily Dynes & Alison Snepp

Photography by Andrew Elton
Styling by Louise Owens

BayBooks
An imprint of HarperCollins*Publishers*

A Bay Books Publication

Bay Books, an imprint of
HarperCollins*Publishers*
25 Ryde Road, Pymble, Sydney, NSW 2073, Australia
31 View Road, Glenfield, Auckland 10, New Zealand

First published in Australia by Bay Books in 1993

Project designs © Alison Snepp 1993
Names text © Cecily Dynes 1993

National Library of Australia
Cataloguing-in-Publication data:

Dynes, Cecily.
    Babies' names & embroidery.
    ISBN 186378 055 5.

    1.names, Personal–Dictionaries. 2.Embroidery – Patterns.

    3.Infants – Clothing – Patterns. I.Snepp, Alison. II. Title
929.4403

Photographer: Andrew Elton
Stylist: Louise Owens
Special thanks to models: Lauren and Patrick
Printed by Griffin Press, Adelaide
Printed in Australia
5 4 3 2 1
97 96 95 94 93

CONTENTS

EMBROIDERY PROJECTS

The arrival of a new baby is one of the most exciting events in life, and is always greeted with an enthusiastic group of family and friends keen to give a gift which is practical and yet attractively personal.

Babies' Names and Embroidery provides a selection of alphabets and a range of projects which will enable an exquisite collection of special gifts to be made from a very elegant christening dress to a practical bib — there are projects for different levels of embroidery skill, and practical things for mothers.

The instructions are comprehensive with full directions for embroidery stitch techniques as well as finishing instructions to make the completion of the project smooth and easy.

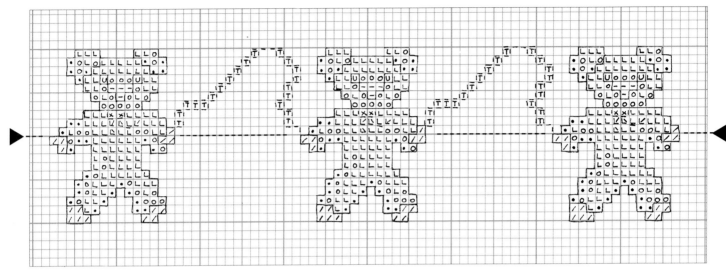

Section 1

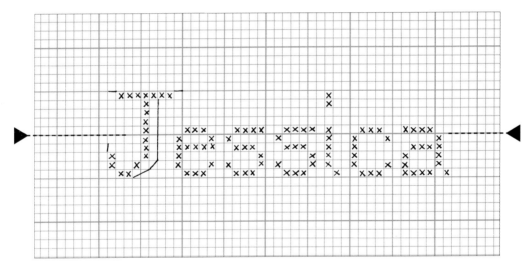

Section 2

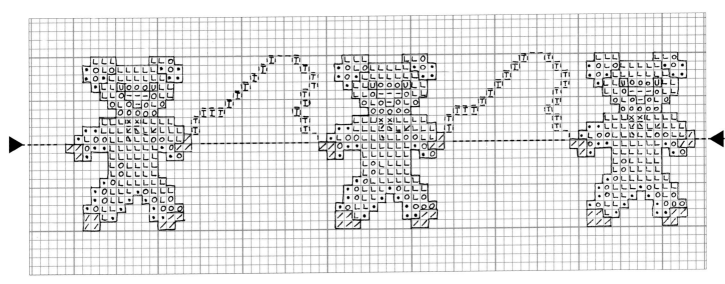

Section 3

LAYOUT PLAN

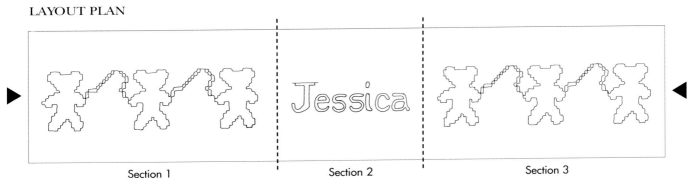

Section 1   Section 2   Section 3

See layout plan for the correct way to join sections of the graph together.
Use the horizontal centre lines to align sections 1, 2 & 3.

One square on the chart represents one cross stitch.
Each cross stitch is worked over one bundle of threads
on the Aida band.

KEY		
Back stitch	Cross stitch	DMC
Γ	✕	961
	T	963
	╱	3041
	—	3072
	∪	959
	L	504
	o	502
⌐	●	500

EMBROIDERY THREAD

Work with a length of embroidery thread which is about 50 cm (20 in) long.

The Baby's Bib has a specially-woven Aida panel in which to work the cross stitch.

MATERIALS

- *Baby's Bib DMC Article BB6785, Banana Ice Colour*
- *DMC Stranded Cotton Article 117, 1 skein each of the following colours: 208, 209, 211, 349, 350, 351, 353, 550, 740, 741, 742, 743, 3051, 3052*
- *Tapestry needle, size 24*
- *Machine thread in a medium colour*
- *Embroidery scissors*

METHOD

1 Carefully count out the number of blocks of thread to find the centre of the Aida panel. At each of the horizontal and vertical centres stitch a row of tacking stitches with the machine thread. With the aid of the arrows at the sides of the chart, rule the centre lines on the graph.

2 Start the embroidery at the centre. This is the point where the ruled lines on the graph and the tacked lines on the fabric intersect. Use two strands of stranded cotton for both the cross stitch and the double running stitch.

Adaptation for other names: Chart the name to be embroidered on the graph paper provided on page 92 using the upper and lower case cross stitch alphabets provided on pages 56–57. The name 'Lauren' uses 44 stitches.

If the name to be embroidered on the bib uses less than 44 stitches on the Aida-woven panel, count the number of stitches required, then find the centre lines on the name and simply embroider the name into the centre of the flowers using the tacked centre lines for placement.

If the name to be embroidered uses more than 44 stitches, chart the name on the graph paper provided on page 92 find only the vertical centre line on the name, and move the embroidery up to where there is more space between the flowers.

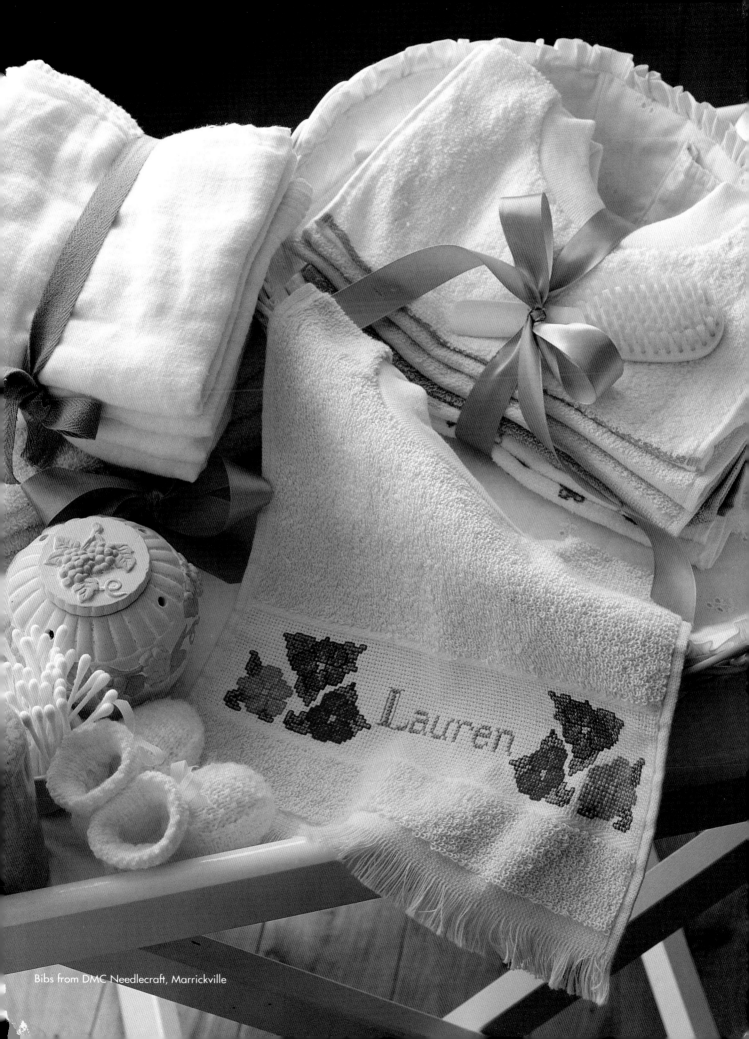

Bibs from DMC Needlecraft, Marrickville

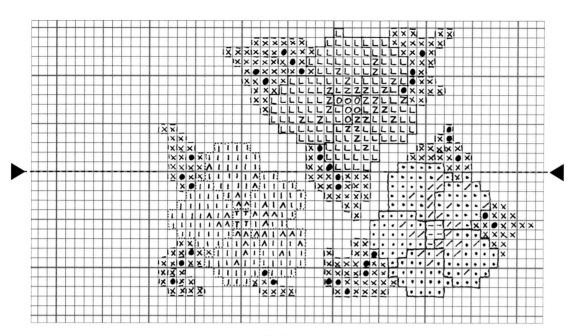

Section 1

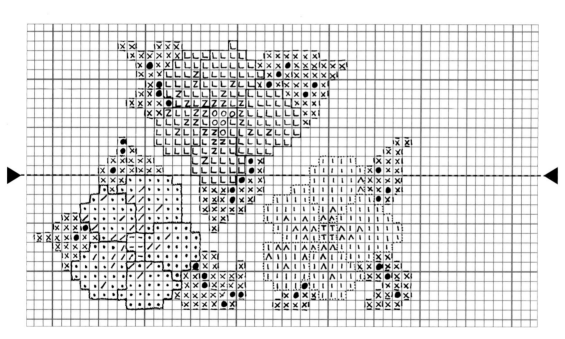

Section 3

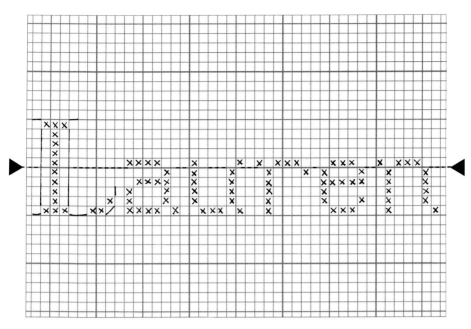

Section 2

LAYOUT PLAN

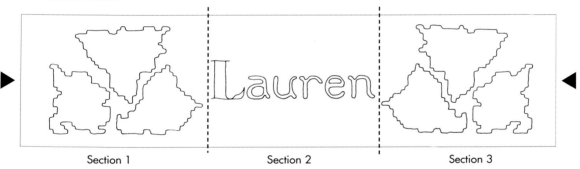

| Section 1 | Section 2 | Section 3 |

See layout plan for the correct way to join sections of the graph together. Use the horizontal centre lines to align sections 1, 2 & 3.

One square on the chart respresents one cross stitch. Each cross stitch is worked over one bundle of threads on the Aida section of the bib.

KEY		
Back stitch	Cross stitch	DMC
	I	741
	∧	742
	T	743
⌐		740
	L	208
	Z	209
	o	211
⌐		550
	•	350
	/	351
	—	353
∫̃		349
	x	3052
	●	3051

David's Nappy Pin Pillow

—————————— ◢ ——————————

Ending Off

Always end off a colour of thread in the back of the same colour for a superior result.

Materials

◆ Square of evenweave linen, 20 cm (8 in), with 10 threads/cm (27 threads/in)
◆ DMC Stranded Cotton Article 117, 1 skein each of the following colours: 702, 791, 817, white
◆ Navy blue medium weight cotton fabric, 30 cm (12 in)
◆ Red medium weight cotton fabric, 30 cm (12 in)
◆ Cotton piping cord, 100 cm (40 in)
◆ Small quantity polyester cushion filling
◆ Tapestry needle, size 24
◆ Machine thread in a medium colour, navy blue and red
◆ Embroidery scissors
◆ Dressmaking pins

Method

1 Oversew by hand or zigzag by machine around the outer edges of the evenweave linen to prevent fraying.

2 Fold the linen in half both ways to find the centre of each side. Tack a line at each of the centre points using machine thread.

3 Find the centre of the graph by ruling lines across and down, connecting the arrows marked on the graph. Start at the centre of the embroidery where the centre lines intersect. Work the cross stitch with two strands of thread.

4 When the embroidery is complete, tack a line, using coloured machine thread, around the outside of the embroidery, 10 threads beyond the outermost edges of the embroidery.

5 **Piping:** Cut two bias strips, each 5 cm (2 in) wide, from the red medium weight cotton (see diagram page 16). Join the bias strips (see diagram page 16). Press the seam open. Fold the bias strip around the piping cord. Stitch the cord into the bias strip using the zipper foot on the sewing machine, making sure that the stitching is very close to the piping cord.

6 Pin the piping to the tacked line around the embroidery, starting halfway along one side of the embroidery. The cord side of the piping should be towards the embroidery and the raw edges of the piping should face outwards towards the oversewn edge of the linen. At the corners, cut the raw edges of the piping a couple of times to make a smooth curve on the piping. Join the ends of the piping together, trimming away any extra fabric and cord. Machine the piping to the embroidery. Remove the tacked lines from the evenweave linen.

7 **Frill:** Cut sufficient strips (on the straight grain) from the navy blue medium weight cotton fabric to make one long strip 120 cm x 12 cm (48 in x 5 in). Join the short ends of the long strip to make one continuous length of frill. Press seams open.

Fold the fabric in half to make one folded piece of fabric 120 cm x 6 cm (48 in x 2½ in). Gather along the raw edges of the fabric frill using the sewing machine set to a straight stitch length of 4 or 5. Pin the frill to the pillow, with the raw edges of the frill facing out towards the raw edge of the evenweave linen. Pull up the gathers to allow the frill to sit smoothly on the piped pillow. When positioning the frill on top of the piping, the stitching line on the frill will be very close to the outer edge of the piping cord. These two seam lines must be matched when pinning the frill into position.

Machine sew the frill and piping to the embroidery, with the zipper foot fitted to the sewing machine, making sure that the stitching is close to the outer edge of the piping cord.

8 **Backing:** Cut a square 20 cm x 20 cm (8 in x 8 in) from the navy blue medium weight cotton fabric. Pin the backing fabric onto the pillow on top of the gathered and positioned frill, taking care that the layers of embroidery, piping and frill remain flat. Machine sew all the layers together leaving a 10 cm (4 in) gap along one side. Trim seam allowances.

Small chest of drawers from Sweet Violets, Lindfield

No of letters length	Evenweave size	Piping cord	Frill
6	23 cm x 23 cm (9 in x 9 in)	110 cm (43 in)	150 cm (60 in)
7	26 cm x 26 cm (10 in x 10 in)	120 cm (47 in)	170 cm (64 in)
8	29 cm x 29 cm (11 in x 11 in)	130 cm (51 in)	180 cm (68 in)
9	32 cm x 32 cm (12 in x 12 in)	140 cm (55 in)	190 cm (72 in)

Turn Nappy Pin Pillow right sides out and fill with polyester cushion filling. Slip stitch the cushion opening closed.

Adaptation for other names: The name 'David' starts and ends with a 'd' and so is ideal for the border of the Nappy Pin Pillow. In order to adapt the design for other names with five letters, but which do not start and end with the same letter, embroider the name along the top and bottom rows of blocks and leave the side blocks without letters on them. Alternatively, work the simple square onto the block as appears on the centre pile of blocks.

For names with less than five letters, reduce the number of blocks in the border. Reposition the centre blocks using the centre lines tacked on the evenweave linen. Sew the piping 25 threads outside the last row of embroidery, and continue to make up the pillow according to the instructions.

For names with more than five letters, the Nappy Pin Pillow will have to be larger. For every letter in the baby's name, add another block across and down the border. Each extra block means that a larger piece of evenweave linen will be required. The table above shows the fabric quantities.

When the baby's name has more than five letters, obtain 2 skeins of white Stranded Cotton. All the materials listed for this project, other than those specified above, remain the same.

To cut bias strips for piping

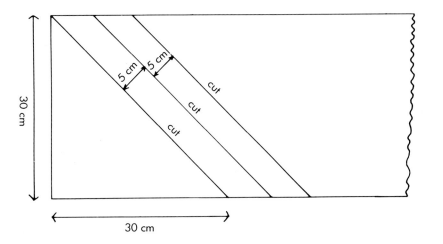

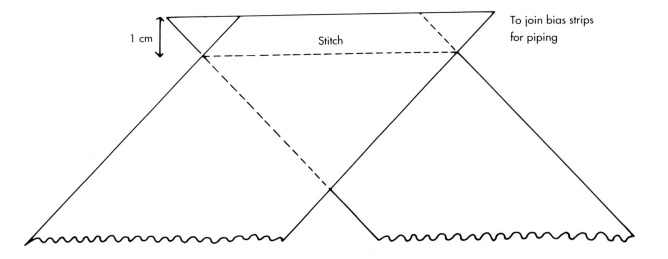

To join bias strips for piping

KEY	
Cross stitch	DMC
I	817
•	white
✗	791
U	702

One square on the chart represents one cross stitch. Each cross stitch is worked over a two thread by two thread square on the evenweave linen.

THE MAIDEN KATE

MATERIALS

- *1 Damask Doll panel DMC Article 2304, colour 1*
- *DMC Stranded Cotton Article 117, 1 skein each of the following colours: 211, 309, 319, 320, 335, 377, 553, 554, 642, 676, 677, 712, 727, 776, 928, 3078, 3326, white*
- *White poplin fabric, 30 cm (12 in)*
- *Polyester cushion filling*
- *Tapestry needle, size 24*
- *White machine thread*
- *Embroidery scissors*
- *Dressmaking pins*

METHOD

The white damask fabric for the doll is woven into Aida sections which are embroidered with cross stitch, and damask sections which are left unstitched. As the Aida sections are woven into the fabric, the embroidery does not need to be centred and the cross stitching may be started anywhere. If the name is not 'Kate', leave the embroidery on the front of the apron until the appropriate name has been charted (see instructions).

1 Embroider the front and back of the doll according to the Aida sections on the damask and the cross stitch chart. Use two strands of thread for the cross stitch.

2 **Assembly of the doll:** Cut two rectangular pieces of white poplin, each the size of a damask panel. Press completed embroidery on the wrong side. Pin a piece of poplin to the wrong side of each embroidered panel.

3 Set the sewing machine to a fine stitch length of 1 or 1.5 and machine sew around the seam line indicated on each panel. Pin the two lined, embroidered panels together, with embroidered sides facing each other, matching the machine stitching lines.

4 Set the machine to sew a normal 2.5 stitch length straight stitch. Machine sew the two panels together using the fine machine stitching lines as a guide. Leave a 12 cm (4½ in) opening along the bottom edge of the doll.

5 Trim seam allowances to 1cm (⅜ in), clip curves and turn the doll right sides out.

6 Fill the doll with polyester cushion filling and slip stitch the bottom edges closed.

Adaptation for other names: The name 'Kate' uses 23 stitches. If the baby's name uses 31 stitches or less, will fit into the panel on the apron. Chart the name on the graph paper provided on page 92 using the lower case cross stitch alphabet on page 57 and embroider the name onto the doll's apron. If the charted name has more than 31 stitches, chart the baby's initials onto the apron instead, using either the upper case or the lower case cross stitch alphabets on pages 56–57.

KEY Cross stitch	DMC
c	211
T	544
I	553
≍	3078
•	727
s	320
∧	319
+	309
–	3326
o	712
/	776
U	335
x	white
■	377
L	928
z	642
◢	676
K	677

THE MAIDEN KATE FRONT

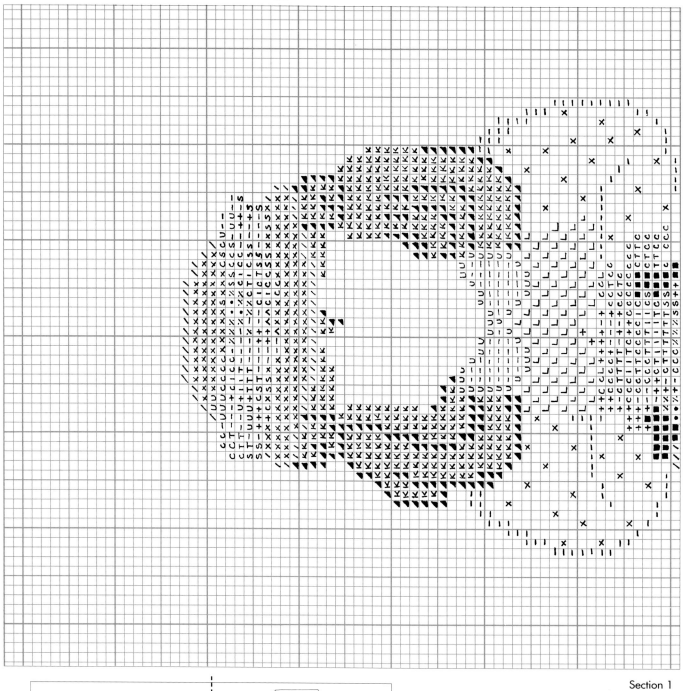

Section 1

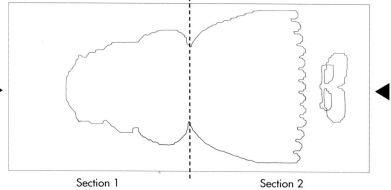

Section 1   Section 2

LAYOUT PLAN

See layout plan for the correct way to join sections of the graph together. Use the arrow heads to align sections 1 and 2.

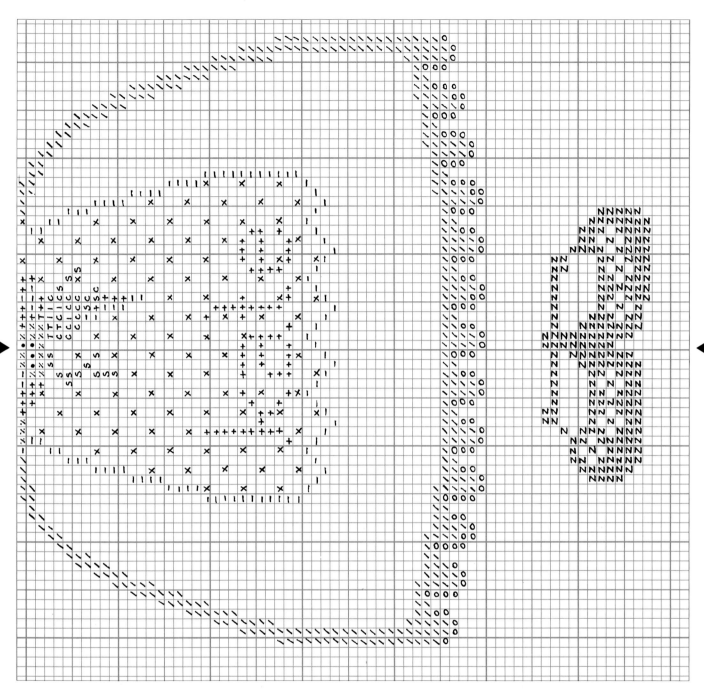

Section 2

One square on the chart represents one cross stitch. Each cross stitch is worked over one bundle of threads in the Aida section.

Refer to colour key on page 18.

THE MAIDEN KATE BACK

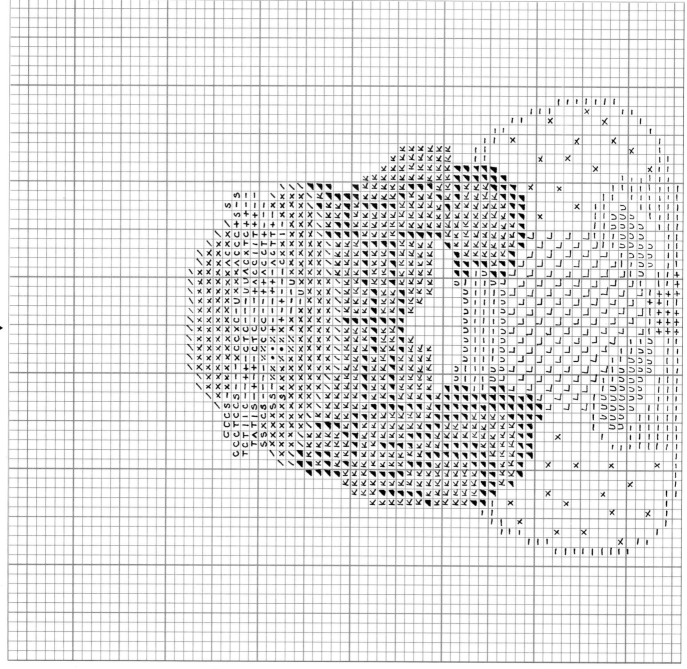

Section 3

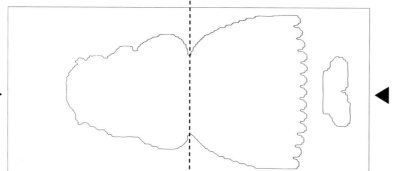

Section 3   Section 4

LAYOUT PLAN

See layout plan for the correct way to join sections of the graph together. Use the arrow headsto align sections 3 and 4.

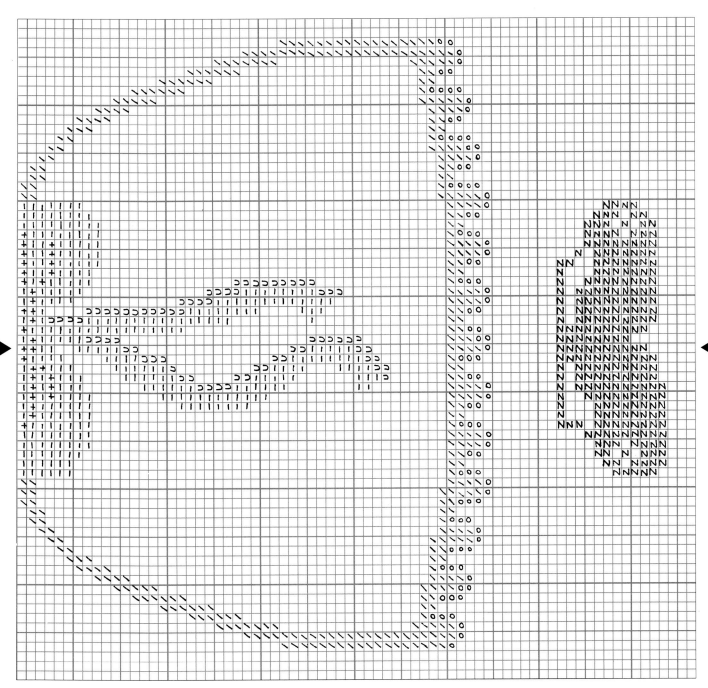

Section 4

One square on the chart represents one cross stitch. Each cross stitch is worked over one bundle of threads in the Aida section.

Refer to colour key on page 18.

$\mathcal{S}$OFT TOYS

It is important to stuff soft toys to give them a cuddly feel and appearance. Make sure you use the correct amount of stuffing. Too little will leave the toy looking shapeless and it won't sit or stand properly. Too much and it will be too hard and not very cuddly and its seams may burst.

The best filling to use is polyester fibre. It is lightweight and very easy to use. It is especially effective when the weight of the toy is important such as for babies' toys. Also, polyester fibre is washable.

Take care to stuff the toy properly the first time as correcting a badly stuffed toy can be difficult. First, tease the fibres or foams into small portions. Push them one at a time into the furthest corners of the toy and work back toward the opening. Using a stuffing stick, push the material firmly into tight corners. Make sure there are no gaps by moulding the toy as you go. Check the feel of the stuffing and adjust its firmess depending on the toy. Leave the stuffed toy to settle for a while before closing it up.

The most suitable stitch for closing the toy is ladder stitch, giving it a secure closure and an almost invisible finish. Begin at one end of the opening and take a few stitches as shown, alternating right to left with left to right stitches (see diagram). Pull up the thread quite tightly to close the part of the hole already stitched. Continue like this until the hole is closed. Fasten threads off securely.

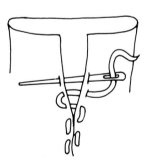

Ladder Stitch

ALEXANDER AND THE ELEPHANTS

STRANDED COTTON

STRANDED COTTON

Divide stranded cotton into its 6 separate strands. Allow each strand to untwist and hang easily. Then put together the number of threads specified in the project instructions. The cotton will cover better and the stitches will look neater.

MATERIALS

- *1 panel Anne Cloth DMC Article 7563, Colour 51*
- *DMC Stranded Cotton Article 117 in the following colours and quantities: 5 skeins 727, 2 skeins 824, 2 skeins 825, 5 skeins 826, 2 skeins 828*
- *Tapestry needle, size 22*
- *Machine thread in ecru and a medium colour*
- *Embroidery scissors*

METHOD

Each square on the Anne Cloth which is to be embroidered will have to have vertical and horizontal centre lines tacked onto it with the medium coloured machine thread. Use three strands of Stranded Cotton for all the embroidery.

1 Start the cross stitch embroidery at the centre of each square on the Anne Cloth.

2 Embroider the Baby Wrap Shawl according to the diagram on page 33.

3 Work the large blue elephants alternately on the centre two rows of the panel.

4 **Hem stitching**: Hem stitch around the outer blue woven line on the fabric according to the hem stitching instructions (see diagrams page 54). Fray the extra fabric outside the hem stitching line to give the shawl a fringed finish.

Adaptation for other names: One panel of Anne Cloth is 9 squares by 6 squares, and the name 'Alexander' has nine letters, each of which fits into a square along the long side. For names with less than nine letters, decide how they will fit across the panel. Any extra squares beyond the name may be left blank, or may have just the border of yellow elephants worked into them.

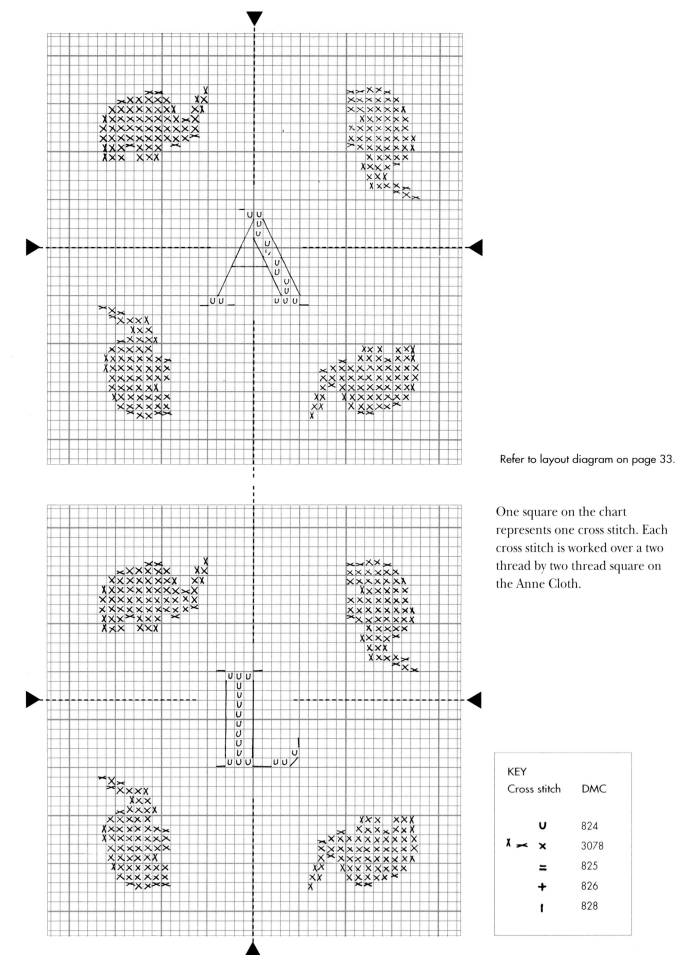

Refer to layout diagram on page 33.

One square on the chart represents one cross stitch. Each cross stitch is worked over a two thread by two thread square on the Anne Cloth.

KEY
Cross stitch   DMC

U   824
x   3078
=   825
+   826
I   828

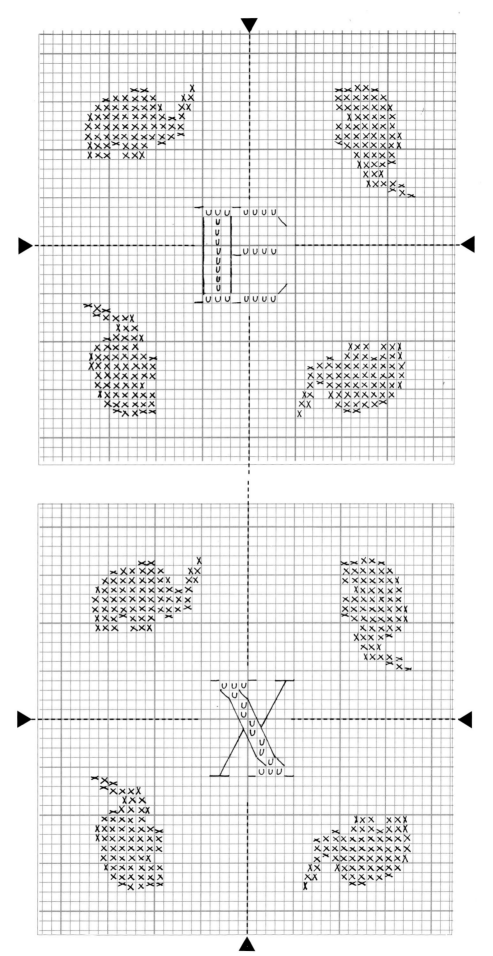

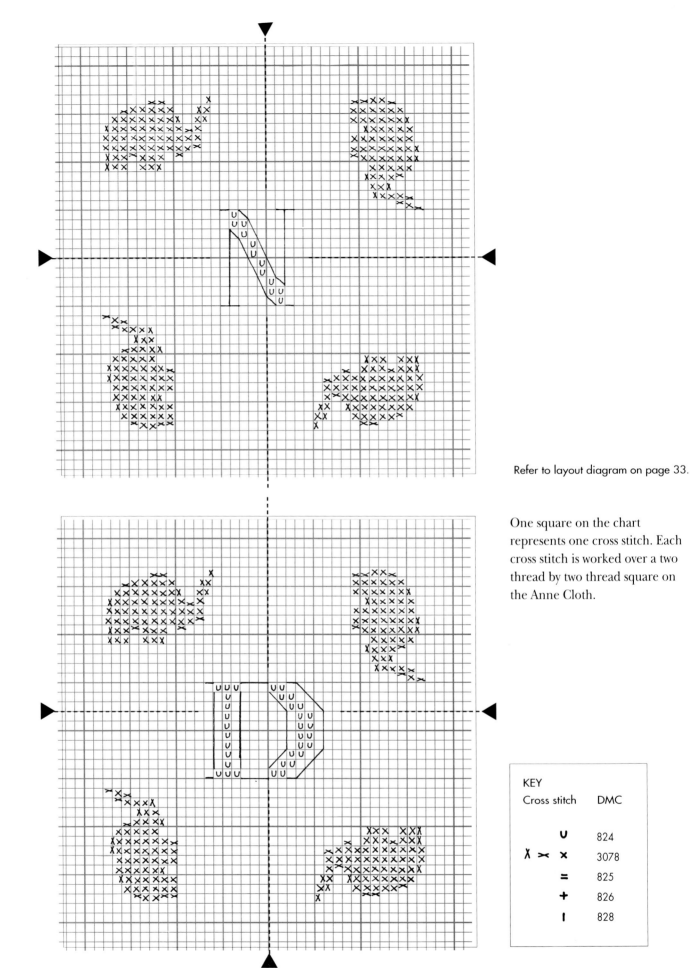

Refer to layout diagram on page 33.

One square on the chart represents one cross stitch. Each cross stitch is worked over a two thread by two thread square on the Anne Cloth.

KEY

Cross stitch	DMC
U	824
X ✕ ✗	3078
=	825
+	826
I	828

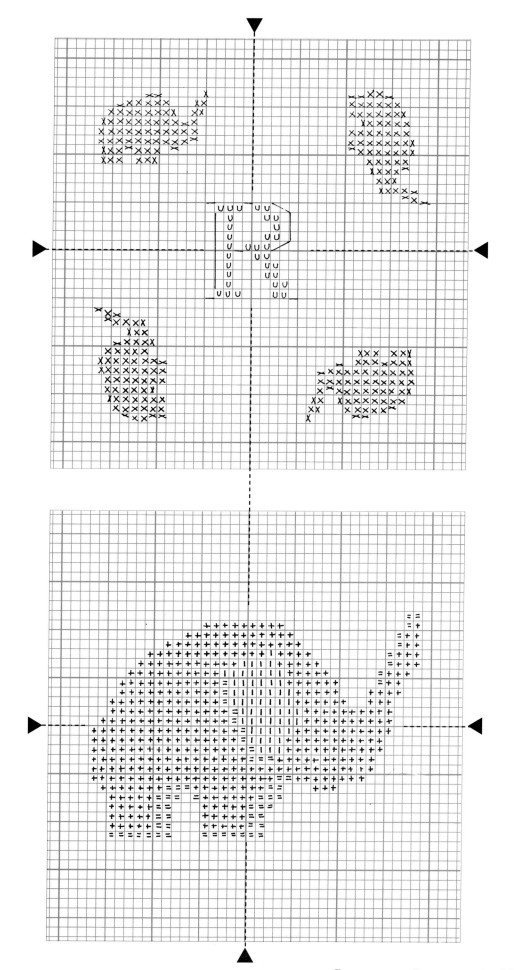

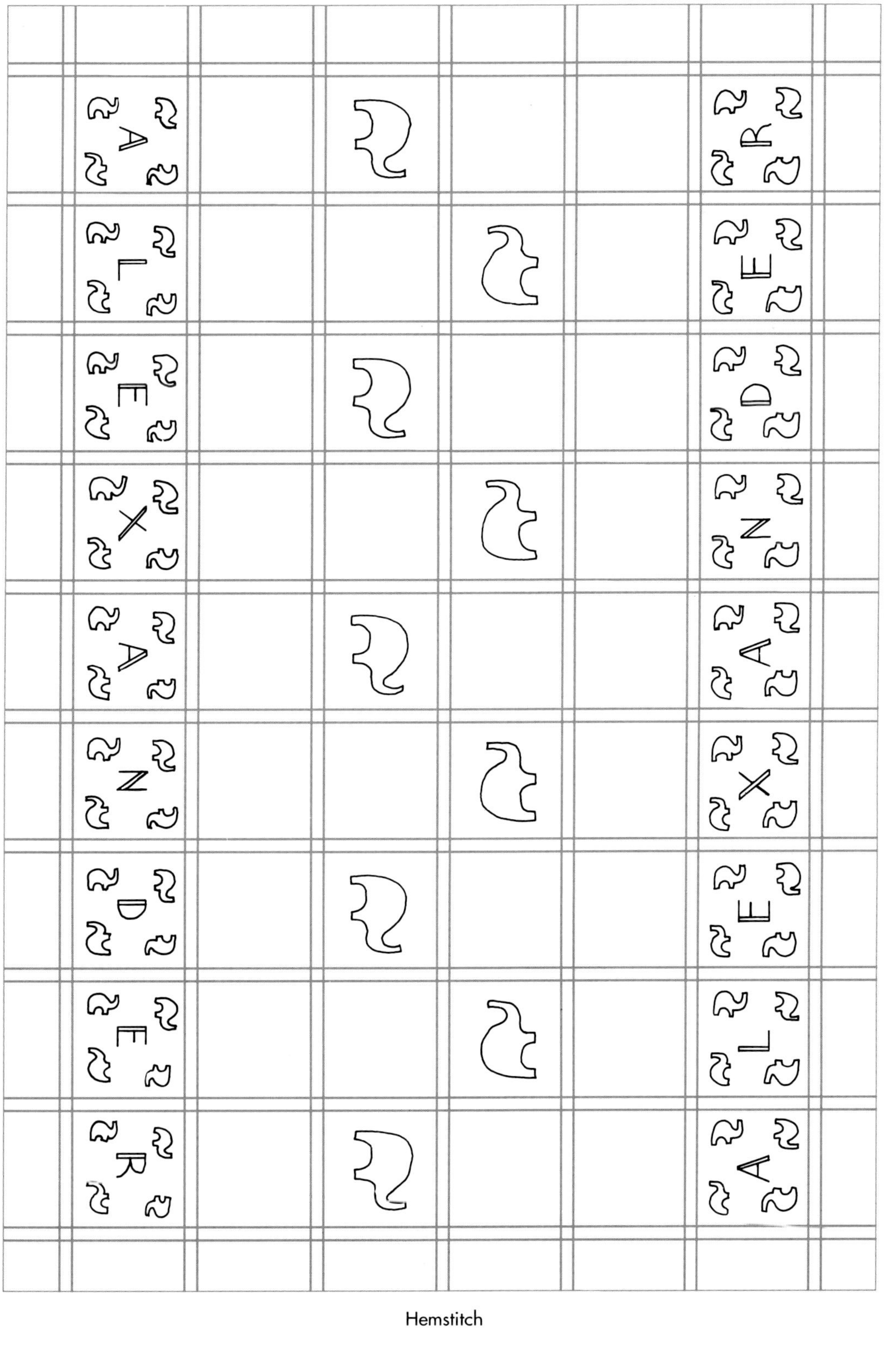

Fringe outer row of squares beyond hemstitching

A

L

E

X

A

N

D

E

R

R

E

D

N

A

X

E

L

A

Hemstitch

LAYOUT PLAN

ELEGANT ELIZABETH

✦

MATERIALS

- ◆ *McCall's pattern 5195 Christening Dress Pattern*
- ◆ *White cotton voile, 150 cm x 140 cm (60 in x 54 in)*
- ◆ *White cotton lace, 100 cm x 2.5 cm (40 in x 1 in)*
- ◆ *White cotton lace, 150 cm x 1 cm (60 in x ⅜ in)*
- ◆ *3 reels Mettler Metrosene Plus Article 1171, white colour*
- ◆ *DMC Stranded Cotton Article 117, 1 skein white*
- ◆ *Embroidery hoop, 6–8 cm (2½–3 in) diameter*
- ◆ *Crewel needle, size 9 or 10*
- ◆ *Embroidery scissors*
- ◆ *Dressmaking scissors*
- ◆ *2 mother-of-pearl buttons, approximately 8 mm (⁷⁄₁₆ in) diameter*
- ◆ *White double-sided satin ribbon, 100 cm x 5 mm (40 in x ¼ in)*
- ◆ *Fine dressmaking pins*
- ◆ *Seam gauge or tape measure*
- ◆ *HB pencil*
- ◆ *Sewing machine with a twin needle and pintucking foot*

METHOD

The Christening Dress follows the McCall's 5195 pattern with a few variations. Follow the pattern's instruction sheets in conjunction with the instructions given below.

1 Cut out the following pattern pieces from the white voile fabric: 2, 3, 4, 5 and 8. Follow the grainlines and cutting quantities indicated on the pattern pieces. Cut one bodice piece number 12.

2 **Bodice:** Cut one rectangle 38 cm x 21 cm (15 in x 8 in) from the white cotton voile. Fold it in half to find the centre of the long edge and tack a centre line down the fabric with white machine thread.

3 Measure 3.5 cm (1⅜ in) each side of the centre line and put in a line of pins at this distance from and parallel to the centre line (see diagram page 40).

4 Machine a pintuck following each line of pins. Machine 16 more pintucks outside each of the first pintucks at each side of the unworked centre panel. Each pintuck should be 4 mm (³⁄₁₆ in) from the adjacent pintuck.

5 Position the pattern piece number 12 on the right side of the pintucked bodice panel matching the centre lines. Pin it onto the fabric. Tack around the outside of the pattern piece to transfer the pattern shape to the pintucked fabric, using the white machine thread (do not tack the paper pattern to the fabric). Remove the paper pattern.

6 Trace the three small shadow work flowers (see page 39) onto the centre of the plain section between the pintucks. Embroider the flowers using one strand of Stranded Cotton and the crewel needle according to the shadow work instructions (see diagrams page 53). Put the fabric into the embroidery hoop before commencing the shadow work.

7 Set the sewing machine to a fine straight stitch length of 1 or 1.5. Stitch 5 mm (¼ in) inside the tacked bodice pattern shape to stabilise the pintucks and to prevent the curved edges stretching. Cut out the bodice front along the tacked bodice pattern shape.

8 **Front:** Gather the upper edge of the front pattern piece 2 and follow McCall's pattern instructions for assembling the front of the Christening Dress.

9 **Back:** Follow McCall's pattern instructions for the assembly of the Back of the dress. Use a straight stitch length of 2 for all seams unless indicated otherwise. Lines of gathering should be made with a straight stitch length of 4 or 5. Join the front and back of the dress at the shoulder seams. Trim shoulder seam allowances to 5 mm (¼ in).

Planter boxes and daisy plants from Michele Shennen's Garden Centre; small chest of drawers from Sweet Violets, Lindfield.

10 Sleeves: Gather the cap of the sleeves between the small circles. Pin the 1 cm (⅜ in) white cotton lace to the cuff edge of the sleeve so that the straight edge of the lace is 5 mm (¼ in) above the cut edge of the fabric (see diagram page 40). The right side of the lace should be facing the right side of the voile.

Set the sewing machine to a small zigzag stitch which is 1.5 wide and 1 long. Zigzag the straight edge of the lace to the voile, placing the zigzag stitching along the straight edge of the lace. Fold back the 5 mm seam allowance on the voile behind the rest of the sleeve fabric — the lace will now protrude below the sleeve.

Set the sewing machine to a zigzag stitch which is 1 wide and 1 long. Zigzag exactly along the folded edge of the voile. Trim the 5 mm (¼ in) seam allowance from the voile using embroidery scissors, taking great care not to cut the lace or the sleeve.

Following page 3 of McCall's pattern instructions, sew the sleeves into the Christening Dress.

11 Bodice facing: Join the front of the bodice facing to the two back pieces of the bodice facing at the shoulder seams. Trim seam allowances to 5 mm (¼ in).

Position the facing inside the bodice with wrong sides together. Turn up the lower edge of the bodice facing to fit neatly behind the seam joining the bodice to the skirt.

Turn in the sleeve edges of the bodice facing to fit neatly alongside the sleeve seams. Slip stitch the facing into position. Note that the neck edge of the facing and the neck edge of the bodice will not be turned in, simply tack the two layers of voile together around the neck edge.

12 Neckline: Cut a length of 1 cm (⅜ in) wide lace twice the length of the neckline seam. Neatly turn in and hem the cut edges of the lace. Some laces have a gathering thread made into the lace, so find the gathering thread, or sew a small hand running stitch along the straight edge of the lace, using machine thread.

Pull up the gathers of the lace to fit the neck edge and position the gathered straight edge of the lace 1 mm ($\frac{1}{32}$ in) above the stitching line around the neck edge of the bodice, with the wrong side of the lace facing the right side of the voile.

13 Cut a bias strip from the leftover voile 35 cm (14 in) long and 3 cm (1¼ in) wide. Fold the strip in half lengthwise and tack the raw edges together along the length of the strip. Press the bias strip.

Position the folded bias strip around the neck edge of the bodice, with the folded side of the bias strip towards the dress and the cut edges towards the cut neck edge. A seam allowance of 5 mm (¼ in) has been allowed on the folded bias strip, so the strip should be positioned to match its seam line, with the seam line around the neck edge of the bodice. The seam joining the bias strip should just include the gathered straight edge of the lace. Machine the bias strip into place. Trim the seam allowance around the neck edge to 3 mm (⅛ in).

Turn the bias strip to the inside of the bodice and slip stitch the folded edge of the bias strip to the stitching line.

14 Buttons and buttonhole loops: Sew one button to the back opening of the Christening Dress just below the lace. Sew the other button onto the back opening just above the seam joining the bodice to the skirt. Work two buttonhole loops (see diagrams page 41) onto the other side of the back opening to fit the buttons.

15 Side and underarm seams: Sew a French seam (see diagram page 40) matching notches, underarm seams and lower edges, to join the side and underarm seam on each side of the dress.

16 Sleeve Cuff Casing: Make the casing at the cuff of the sleeves. Cut 2 bias strips from the leftover voile, each 32 cm (12½ in) long and 2 cm (¾ in) wide. Turn in 5 mm (¼ in) along each long edge of each strip and tack back the turning. Press the bias strips.

17 Position one bias strip on each sleeve 1 cm (⅜ in) from the join of lace and voile, with

wrong sides of bias strip and sleeve together. Start the bias strip 3mm (⅛ in) to one side of the underarm seam, pin the strip around the sleeve and finish the bias strip 3 mm (⅛ in) to the other side of the underarm sleeve. Machine the bias strips into position, stitching about 1 mm ($\frac{1}{32}$ in) from each long edge of the bias strips, leaving the ends unstitched.

18 Finishing the hem of the dress: Position the straight edge of the 2.5 cm (1 in) wide lace 5 mm (¼ in) above the lower edge of the skirt, with right sides facing and pin into place (see diagram page 40). Join the two ends of the lace to fit, using a small hand running stitch.

Set the sewing maching to a fine zigzag stitch which is 1.5 wide and 1 long. Zigzag along the straight edge of the lace, joining it to the bottom of the skirt. Fold the 5 mm (¼ in) seam allowance back behind the body of the skirt so that the lace protrudes below the voile.

Set the sewing machine to a zigzag stitch which is 1 wide and 1 long and zigzag along the join between the voile and the lace. Trim away the 5 mm (¼ in) seam allowance from the voile using embroidery scissors. Take great care not to cut the lace or the skirt while trimming the seam allowance.

19 Shadow embroidery around the hem of the dress: Find the centre of the front skirt of the Christening Dress. Measure 7 cm (2¾ in) up from the join between the wide lace and the hem of the skirt. Tack a line around the hem of the skirt which is 7 cm (2¾ in) from the join.

Position the ruled centre lines of the 'Elizabeth' drawing (see diagram page 39) beneath the skirt, matching it to the centre line which has been tacked around the hem of the skirt. Trace the lettering very lightly onto the right side of the voile with the HB pencil.

Embroider the lettering with one strand of Stranded Cotton in the crewel needle, placing the fabric in the embroidery hoop before starting the shadow embroidery.

Work out how many repeats of the ribbon and

flower (diagram page 39) can be worked around the skirt either side of the baby's name. Each interval between each ribbon and flower pattern will be approximately 6 cm (2⅛ in), but the actual interval will be determined by the size of the Christening Dress.

20 Skirt pintucks: Put in a line of pins 4.5 cm (1¾ in) above the join between the lace and the skirt all around the skirt. Set the machine up to pintuck and stitch one pintuck along the line of pins. Stitch 6 more pintucks below the first at 4 mm (³⁄₁₆ in) intervals (7 pintucks altogether).

21 Finishing the cuffs: Cut two 50 cm (20 in) lengths from the white satin ribbon. Thread one length of ribbon through each sleeve casing. Using ribbon in the sleeve casing makes the sleeves of the Christening Dress easy to iron.

Note: It is easier to dress the baby before the cuffs are drawn up along the ribbon. When the ribbon has been drawn up around the baby's wrists, tie the ends of the ribbon together into a bow and tuck the ends out of sight into the sleeve of the dress.

22 Buttonhole loops: Make the buttonhole loops on the opposite side of the bodice opening to where the buttons have been attached.

Thread a doubled length of white machine thread into the crewel needle and tie a small knot at the end of the thread. Pull the knot into the space between the bodice and its facing, bringing the needle up at the edge of the bodice.

Take a stitch about 8 mm (⁷⁄₁₆ in) below where the thread was fastened into the fabric (see diagram 1, page 41) and leave a loop of thread protruding from the fabric which will fit comfortably around the button. Take another stitch into the edge of the bodice at the same place where the thread came out of the fabric (see diagram 2, page 41). Pull the stitch through until the loops are the same size and will fit the button comfortably.

Pass the needle under the loops just made, with the thread behind the needle, and pull the thread securely around the thread loop (see diagram 3, page 41). Pass the needle under the loops again, with the thread behind the needle, and continue in this manner until the thread loops are covered with the buttonhole stitch (see diagram 4, page 41).

Adaptation for other names: For names other than 'Elizabeth', trace the letters of the name onto a sheet of tracing paper using the upper and lower case alphabets for surface stitchery on pages 58–59. Measure the distance the name takes and find the centre. Position the traced name behind the voile as described in the section 'Shadow embroidery around the hem of the dress', matching the centre lines, and lightly trace the name onto the skirt using the HB pencil. Work out how many repeats of the ribbon and flower pattern will fit around the hem of the dress and embroider the shadow work.

SHADOW WORK FLOWERS FOR BODICE

RIBBON AND FLOWER PATTERN FOR HEM OF SKIRT

NAME FOR HEM OF SKIRT

PINTUCKING PLAN FOR BODICE

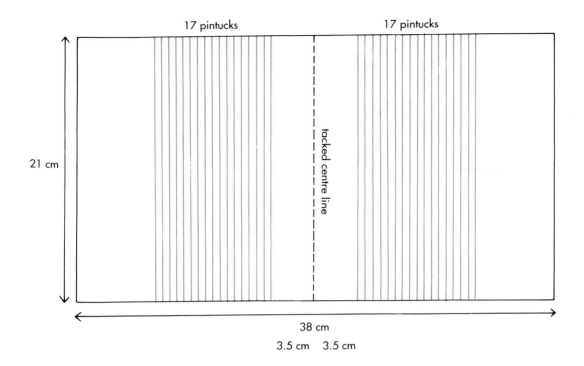

17 pintucks   17 pintucks

tacked centre line

21 cm

38 cm

3.5 cm   3.5 cm

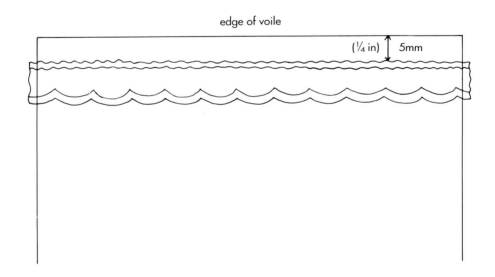

edge of voile

(¼ in) 5mm

POSITIONING OF LACE ON CUFF AND HEM

1

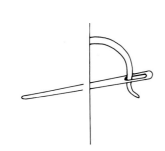

2

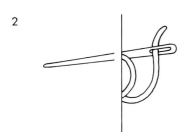

3

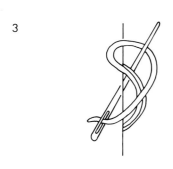

4

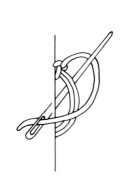

BUTTONHOLE LOOPS

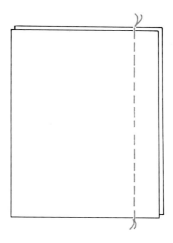

First part: With right sides together and a 5mm (¼ in) seam allowance, sew the first seam. Trim the seam allowance to 3mm (⅛ in). Press seam flat.

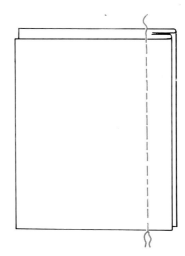

Second part: With right sides together and a 8mm (⅜ in) seam allowance, sew the second seam. Press seam flat.

BENJAMIN AT THE BEACH

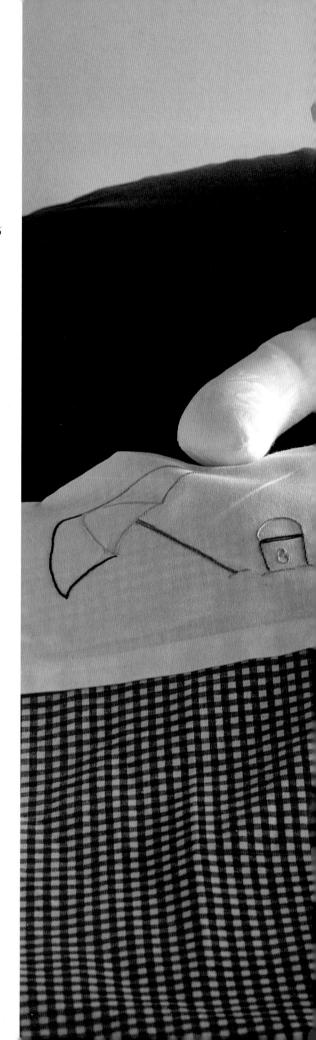

STICKY NEEDLE

If a needle tends to stick when it is pulled through fabric, run the needle through your hair and it won't stick anymore.

MATERIALS

- *White cotton sheeting, 150 cm x 115 cm (63 in x 45 in)*
- *DMC Stranded Cotton Article 117, 1 skein each of the following colours: 307, 502, 676, 702, 725, 742, 809, 824, 890, 917, 959, 991, 3046*
- *Embroidery hoop 15–20 cm (6–8 in) diameter*
- *Crewel needle, size 7 or 8*
- *White machine thread*
- *Embroidery scissors*
- *HB pencil*
- *Dressmaking pins*

METHOD

1 Turn in a doubled hem 1 cm (⅜ in) wide down each long side of the sheet. Pin, then machine with a straight stitch, or hem by hand using the white machine thread. Turn in each short end of the sheet with a doubled hem 2 cm (¾ in) wide. Pin, then machine the hem or hem by hand.

2 Find the centre of one short end of the sheet and mark with a line of pins. Position the embroidery design underneath the sheet, matching the centre lines on the design with those on the sheet. Trace the design lightly onto the sheet with the HB pencil.

3 Start the embroidery anywhere you wish, placing the section to be embroidered in the embroidery hoop. The fabric should be kept taut in the embroidery hoop while the design is being stitched.

Follow the embroidery key for the colours and embroider all of the design with stem stitch (see diagrams page 54) except for the windows on the right sandcastle which are embroidered with lazy daisy stitch (see chain stitch instructions page 55). All of the embroidery is worked with three strands of Stranded Cotton thread.

4 When the embroidery is complete, press the sheet on the wrong side.

Adaptation for other names: For names other than 'Benjamin' trace the name using the upper and lower case surface stitchery alphabets on pages 58–59. Position the name in between the two sections of the beach scene and embroider the design as set out in the instructions above.

FEATURE	SECTION	DMC
Left umbrella:	top segment	809
	middle segment	959
	lowest segment	890
	pole	502
Bucket:	outline	991
	handle	742
	B	307
Spade:		991
Left sandcastle:	outline	676
	windows and door	3046
	flag	917
Benjamin:		725
Right sandcastle:	outline	676
	windows and door	3046
	flag	917
Left beach ball:		742
		809
		959
Right beach ball:		991
		307
		742
Right umbrella:	top segment	824
	middle segment	702
	lowest segment	959
	pole	502

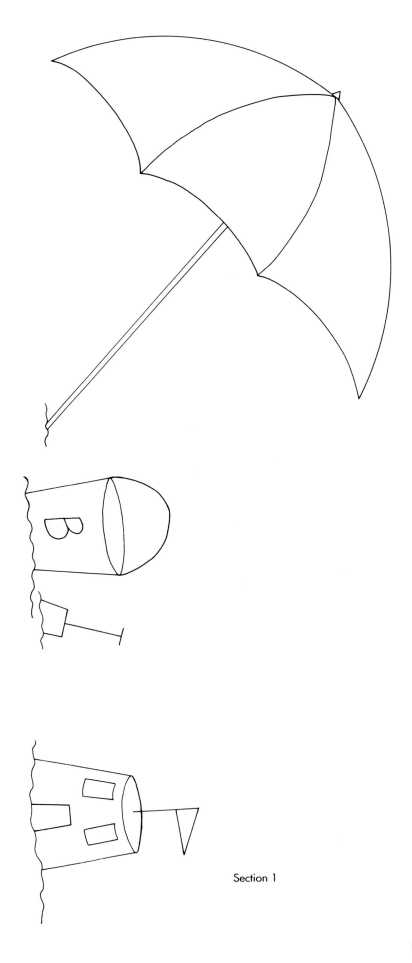

Section 1

Section 2

LAYOUT PLAN

Section 1   Section 2   Section 3

See layout plan for the correct way to join sections of the graph together.

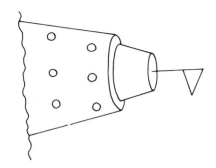

FEATURE	SECTION	DMC
Left umbrella:	top segment	809
	middle segment	959
	lowest segment	890
	pole	502
Bucket:	outline	991
	handle	742
	B	307
Spade:		991
Left sandcastle:	outline	676
	windows and door	3046
	flag	917
Benjamin:		725
Right sandcastle:	outline	676
	windows and door	3046
	flag	917
Left beach ball:		742
		809
		959
Right beach ball:		991
		307
		742
Right umbrella:	top segment	824
	middle segment	702
	lowest segment	959
	pole	502

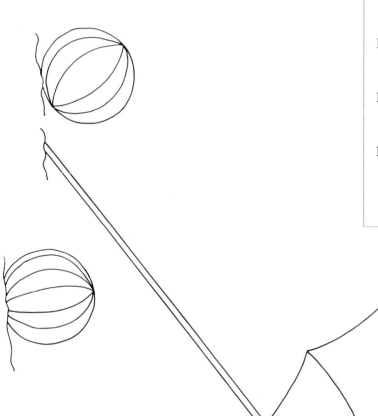

MATTHEW AND THE MOUSE

MATERIALS

- *White cotton sheeting 130 cm x 40 cm (52 in x 16 in)*
- *DMC Stranded Cotton Article 117, 1 skein each of the following colours: 224, 451, 645, 935, 3064, 3772, 3773*
- *Embroidery hoop, 7–10 cm (3–4 in) diameter*
- *Crewel needle, size 7 or 8*
- *White machine thread*
- *HB pencil*
- *Embroidery scissors*
- *Dressmaking pins*

METHOD

1 Turn in a 1 cm (⅜ in) double hem on each short end of the sheeting. Pin and machine sew the hem with a straight stitch.

2 Fold the sheeting into three sections (as shown). Machine sew with a straight stitch along the long sides of the folded pillowcase. Zigzag the raw edges of the pillowslip to prevent fraying. Turn the pillowslip right sides out and press.

3 Lightly trace the embroidery design into the top left corner of the pillowslip using the HB pencil.

4 Place the fabric into the embroidery hoop at the point where the embroidery is to begin and embroider the design according to the key below. All of the embroidery is worked with two strands of thread.

Note: The fur of the mouse is embroidered with two strands of Stranded Cotton in the needle, but the strands are of different colours (the key shows which colours are mixed).

The straight stitches which represent the mouse's fur should be made of varying length, and the three colour combinations can be worked at random around the mouse's body and tail to give a 'furry' look. While embroidering the fur, it is a good idea to have the design drawing close by and to refer regularly to the direction of the fur to help with the embroidery.

Adaptation for other names: For names other than 'Matthew', trace the letters from the upper and lower case surface stitchery alphabets on pages 58–59. Trace the mouse on the upper left of the beginning of the name and embroider the pillowcase as described.

MAKING UP A PILLOW CASE

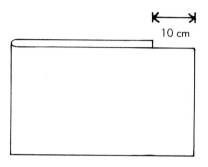

Right sides together

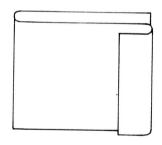

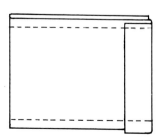

1 cm seam allowance

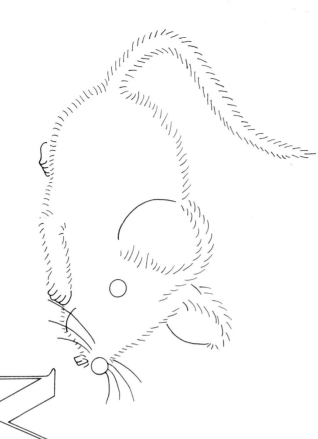

Matthew

Section	Stitch	DMC
Matthew:	chain stitch	935
Mouse's ears:	stem stitch	224
Mouse's feet:	stem stitch	224
Mouse's nose:	stem stitch	645
Mouse's eye:	stem stitch	645
Mouse's whiskers:	stem stitch	645
Mouse's fur:	straight stitch	451 + 3772 3064 + 3772 3773 + 3064

STITCH
INSTRUCTIONS

The thorough step-by-step

stitch instructions on the next pages

will guide you through all stitches

used in the projects.

Cross stitch 1

Cross stitch 2

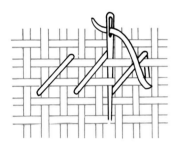

Cross stitch 3

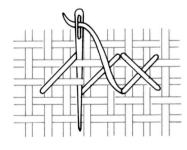

Cross stitch 4

Cross stitch

It is important when working cross stitch that each stitch is worked in the same manner so that the second part of the cross stitch is always in the same direction. Use a tapestry needle for all cross stitch in this book.

Bring the needle up through the fabric at the lower left hand side of the stitch. Count over two threads of linen (or one bundle of Aida fabric) to the right and two threads (one bundle) up and put the needle into the fabric at this point. In the same movement, count two threads (one bundle) directly down and bring the needle out through the fabric. This is a half a cross stitch (see diagram Cross stitch 1). Count to the right over two threads (one bundle) from where the top of the last stitch went into the fabric and put the needle in here, bringing it out two threads (one bundle) below. (See diagram Cross stitch 2.)

Work along a row in this manner until as many half stitches have been worked as are indicated in that row on the chart.

Without turning the embroidery, work back across the row, crossing each stitch into the same holes as the first half of the cross stitches. (See diagrams Cross stitch 3 and 4.)

Ending off: To end off cross stitch, finish the stitch being worked, take the needle through to the back of the work and then run the needle underneath 5 or 6 vertical stitches on the back of the work (see diagram Ending off cross stitch). If the embroidered project is to be washed frequently, it is a good idea to then run the needle back under 4 verticals to lock the threads more securely.

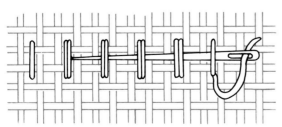

Ending off cross stitch

Half cross stitch

Half cross stitches are worked to give a softer edge to an area of cross stitch. A half cross stitch will be worked over the full stitch in one direction, but only half the stitch in the other direction. One half cross stitch may be two threads (one bundle) high, but only one thread (half a bundle) wide or vice versa. (See diagram Half cross stitch.)

The chart will show exactly which position a half cross stitch should be by the position of the symbol within the square on the graph paper. If a row of cross stitch contains one or more half cross stitches, work these stitches in the row in the normal sequence for the row, both with regard to which part of the cross stitch is worked first and where the half cross stitch(es) lie in the row. Use a tapestry needle for all half cross stitch.

Ending off: End off half cross stitches in the same manner as described for cross stitch.

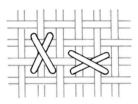

Half cross stitch

Double running stitch (Holbein stitch)

Double running stitch is most useful for outlining areas of cross stitch and for working straight lines as it looks the same on the back as on the front. Use a tapestry needle for all double running stitch.

This stitch is simply a running stitch worked over and under the number of threads or bundles shown on the chart, (see diagram Double running stitch 1). Turn the work around and work the running stitch back to fill in the gaps left on the first pass of running stitch (see diagram Double running stitch 2).

If double running stitch is to be worked as an outline, always work the cross stitch first, then the double running stitch, otherwise the cross stitch will cover the outline.

Ending off: Finish a stitch, take the needle through to the back of the work, and whip over and over through 5 or 6 stitches.

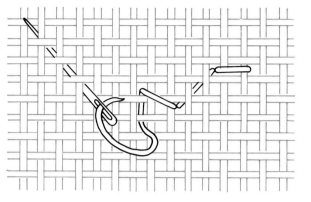

Double running stitch 1

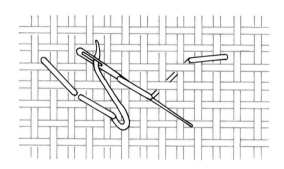

Double running stitch 2

Shadow work

Shadow embroidery is easy to work from the right side of the fabric, using back stitch which is worked alternately from one side to the other in the stitch area. A fine crewel needle (size 9 or 10) and one strand of stranded embroidery thread should be used for shadow embroidery.

Bring the needle up through the fabric, a little distance to the left of the end of one line. Put the needle in at the end of the line (i.e. a little to the right of where the thread comes out of the fabric) (see diagram Shadow work 1). Bring the needle out of the fabric on the other line, a little to the left of the end of

the other line (see diagram Shadow work 1) and put the needle down into the fabric again at the end of the same line (see diagram Shadow work 2).

Bring the needle up again on the first line, a little to the left of the end of the last stitch on the first line (see diagram Shadow work 3) and put the needle down into the fabric again in the same hole where the first back stitch ended (see diagram Shadow work 3).

Continue in this manner, working back stitches alternately on one line and then the other. It is the thread taken from one side to the other which gives the shadow effect.

When working a curved area of shadow embroidery, the back stitches will have to be shorter on the shorter line and longer on the longer line so that the further end of the curved shape is reached at the same time by both sides.

Ending off: Complete a stitch, take the needle through to the back of the work and carefully run the needle through the back of the stitches splitting the embroidery thread behind the back stitches.

Shadow work 1

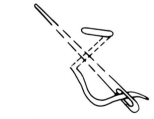

Shadow work 2

Shadow work 3

Hem stitching

Hem stitching is a stitch which is pulled tightly to bring together in bundles the threads around which each stitch is worked. For hem stitching, use a tapestry needle and ecru machine thread.

Bring the needle up through the fabric an even number of threads from a blue line, at the inside of the outermost blue line woven into the fabric (see diagram Hem stitching 1). Leave a starting length of about 9 or 10 cm (4 in) on the back of the work. This end should be ended-off after the length of thread is complete following the ending off instructions. Count to the right over two threads and up two threads and put the needle in here, bringing it out two threads to the left of where the needle went in (see diagram Hem stitching 1).

Put the needle into the fabric, two threads to the right of where the thread comes out (this is the same hole where the last stitch went into the fabric) and bring it out two threads directly below (see diagram Hem stitching 2). Pull thread tightly.

Put the needle into the fabric again, two threads to the right of the top right hand side of the last stitch, bringing it out two threads to the left (see diagram Hem stitching 3). Pull thread tightly. Repeat steps 2 and 3 until the length to be hem stitched is complete.

The even, firm tension on the thread will have to be maintained while hem stitching in order to pull the threads together into bundles.

Ending off: Work a row of running stitches back between the two blue threads around which the hem stitching is worked. The row of running stitches should be under and over about 15 individual threads in the fabric. Starting threads should be finished off in the same manner.

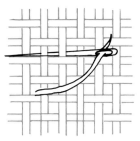

Hem stitching 1

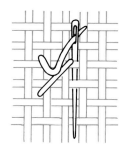

Hem stitching 2

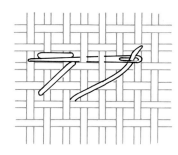

Hem stitching 3

Stem stitch

Stem stitch is an excellent stitch for outlining areas of colour. Use a crewel needle and the number of strands of embroidery thread indicated in the project instructions.

Stem stitch is worked from left to right with the needle pointing to the left. Bring the needle out of the fabric at the start of the line of stitching. Put the needle into the fabric a short distance away and bring it out halfway along the stitch length to the left. Keep down the length of thread running to the needle (See diagram Stem stitch 1).

Put the needle into the fabric again, half a stitch length to the right of where the last stitch ended, and bring the needle up where the stitch before last finished, again keep the length of thread down (see diagram Stem stitch 2). Stitch, following the line in this manner, always keeping the length of thread down to maintain the line of the stitch.

Ending off: Finish a stitch, take the needle to the wrong side of the embroidery and whip over and over the back of about 6 stitches. Pull the thread taut and cut it off close to the embroidery.

Stem stitch 1

Stem stitch 2

Stem stitch 3

Chain stitch

Chain stitch gives an open line stitch or it can be used singly to make a rounded individual stitch.

Bring the needle out of the fabric at the place where the stitching is to start. Take the thread around in a circle ahead of the needle and put the needle into the fabric at the same place as the thread comes out of the fabric. In the same movement, bring the needle out of the fabric in the middle of the circle made by the thread (the thread should be underneath the needle) (see diagram Chain stitch 1). Pull the thread through the fabric smoothly, gently allowing the full loop of the chain stitch to form. Start the next stitch by taking the thread around in a circle, and putting the needle back into the same hole as the thread

comes out of the fabric (see diagram Chain stitch 2).

Continue in the same manner until the end of the row of chain stitch is reached. After the last stitch has been pulled into place, insert the needle into the fabric on the outside of the loop (see diagram Chain stitch 3).

Individual chain stitches, or lazy daisy stitches, may be worked in the same manner. Each stitch is completed by placing the needle into the fabric on the outside of the loop, then ending off at the back, or a nearby stitch is commenced.

Ending off: After finishing the last stitch, the thread should be on the wrong side of the fabric. Finish by stitching over and over through the stitches on the wrong side of the fabric.

Straight stitch

Straight stitches are made up of single stitches working in and out of the fabric in the directions indicated in the embroidery design. Diagrams Straight stitch 1, 2 and 3 show the simple directions for the stitch.

There are only two points to remember with straight stitch: a) keep the length of the stitches random and different and b) keep the interval between the stitches varied.

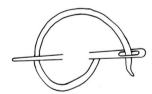

Chain stitch 1

Straight stitch 1

Chain stitch 2

Straight stitch 2

Chain stitch 3

Straight stitch 3

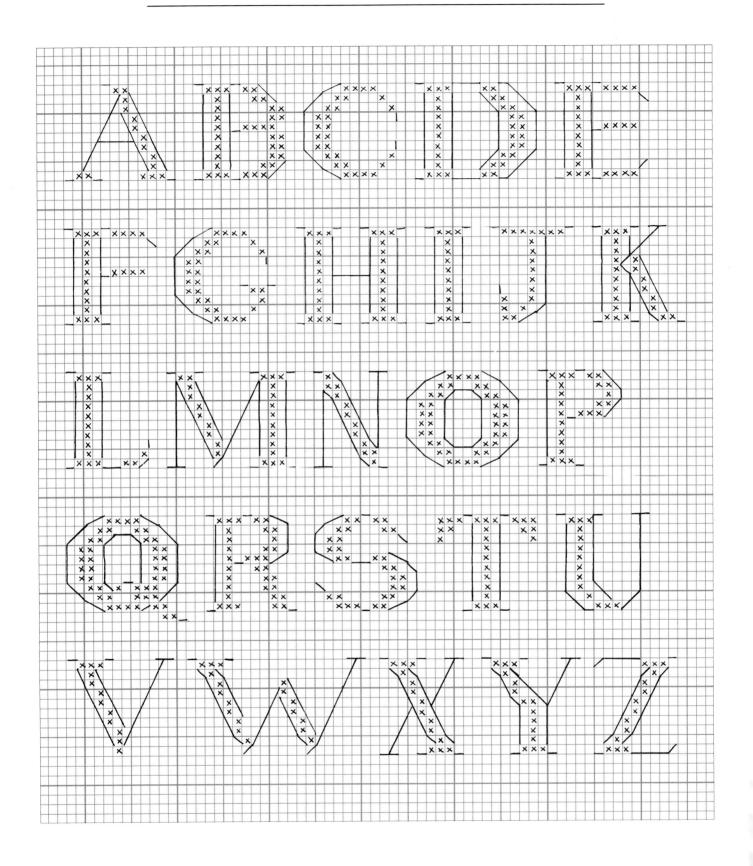

CROSS STITCH ALPHABET LOWER CASE

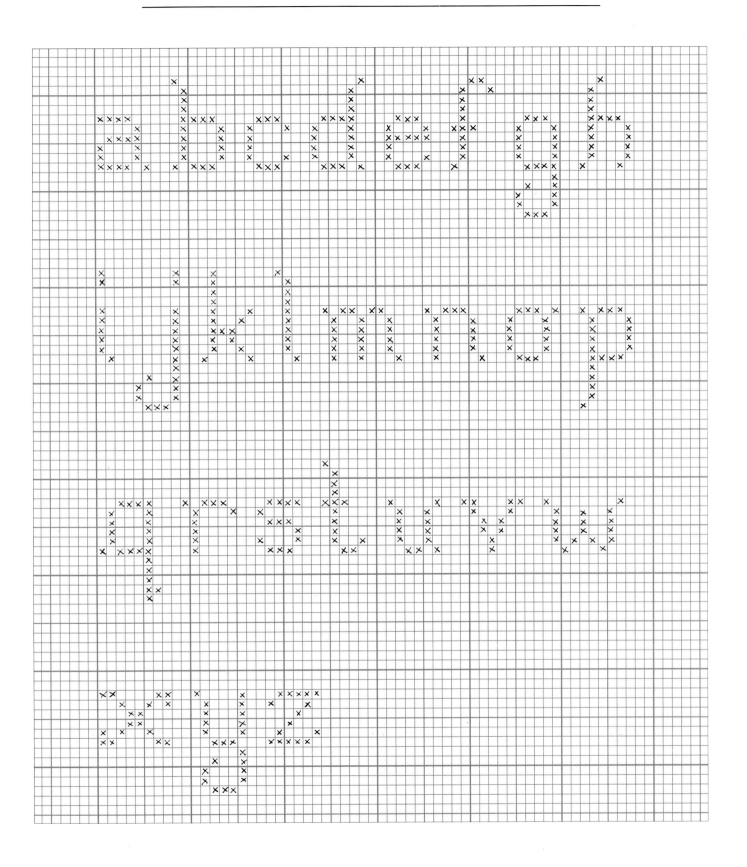

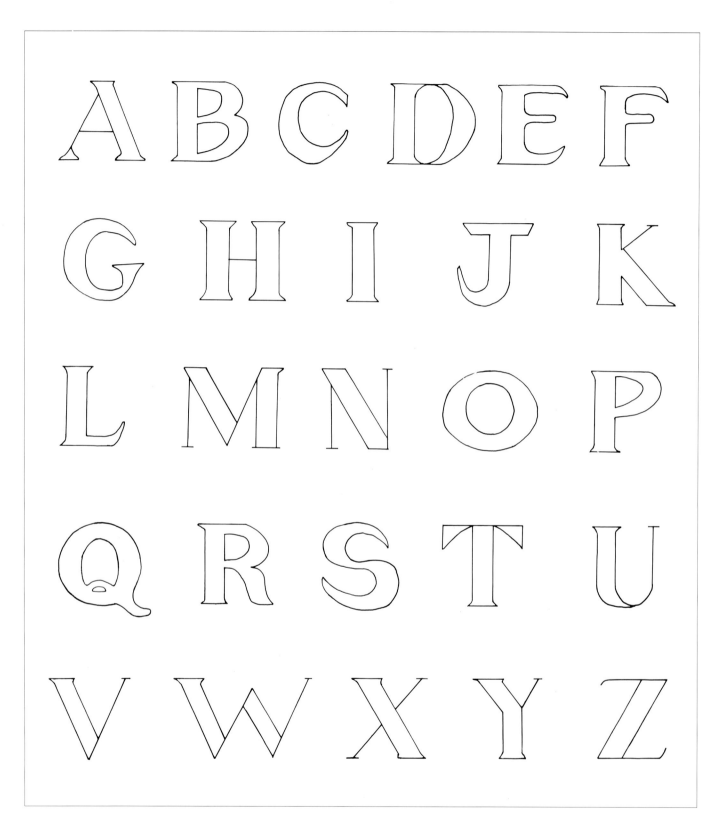

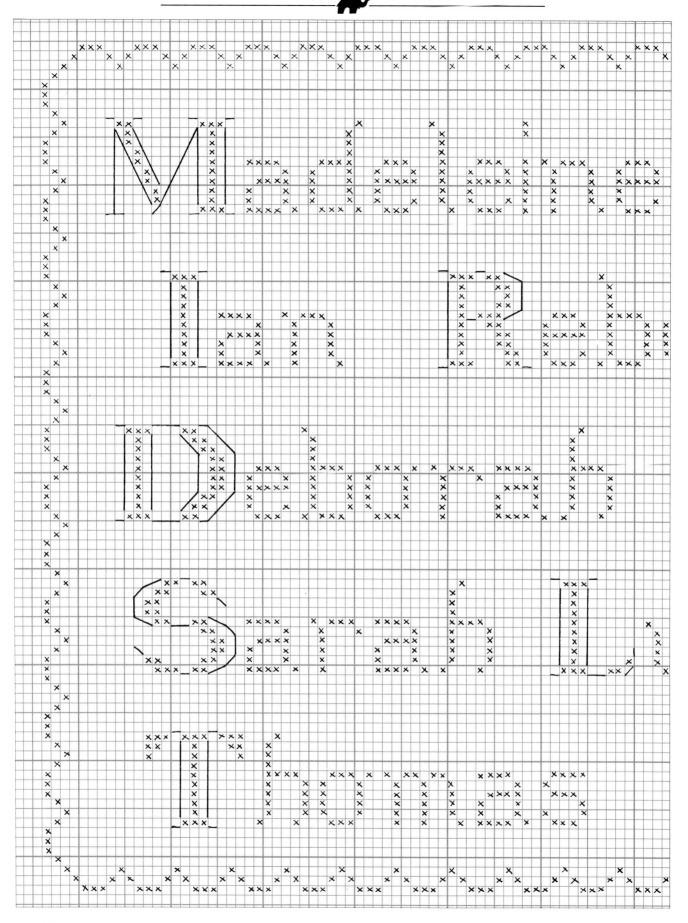

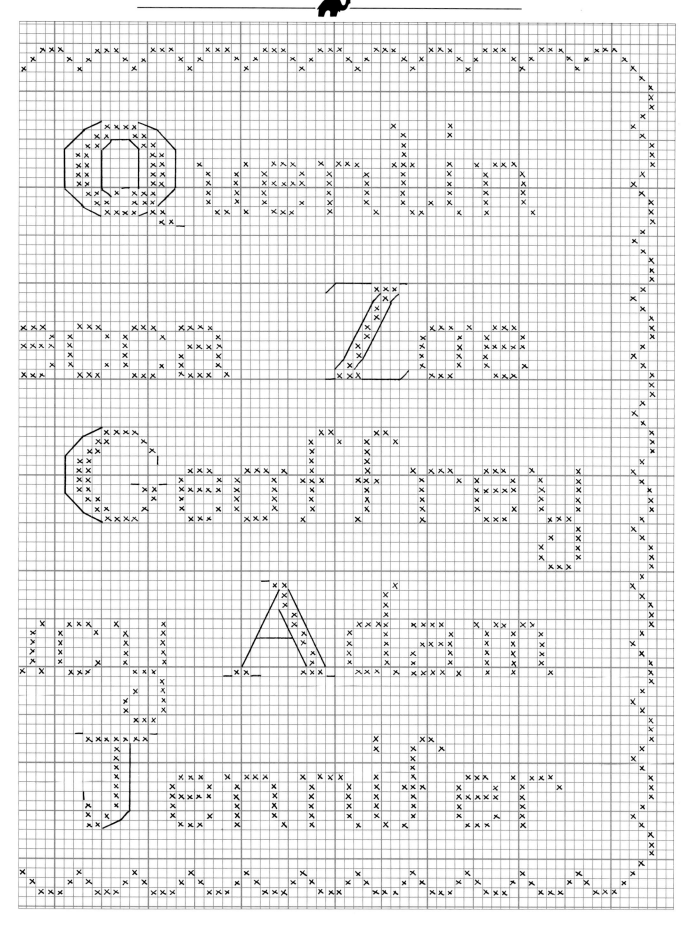

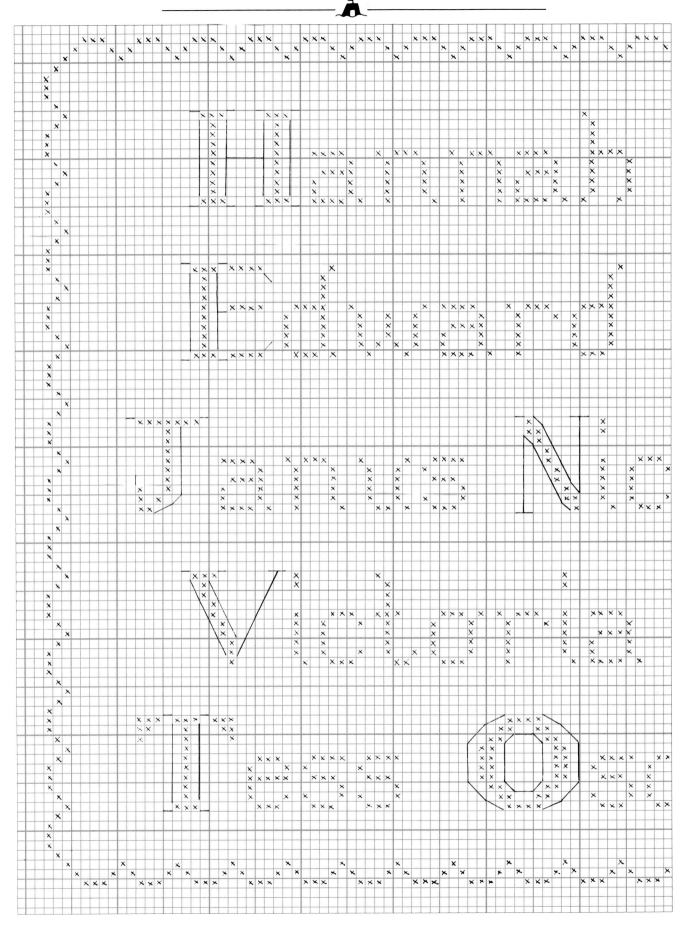

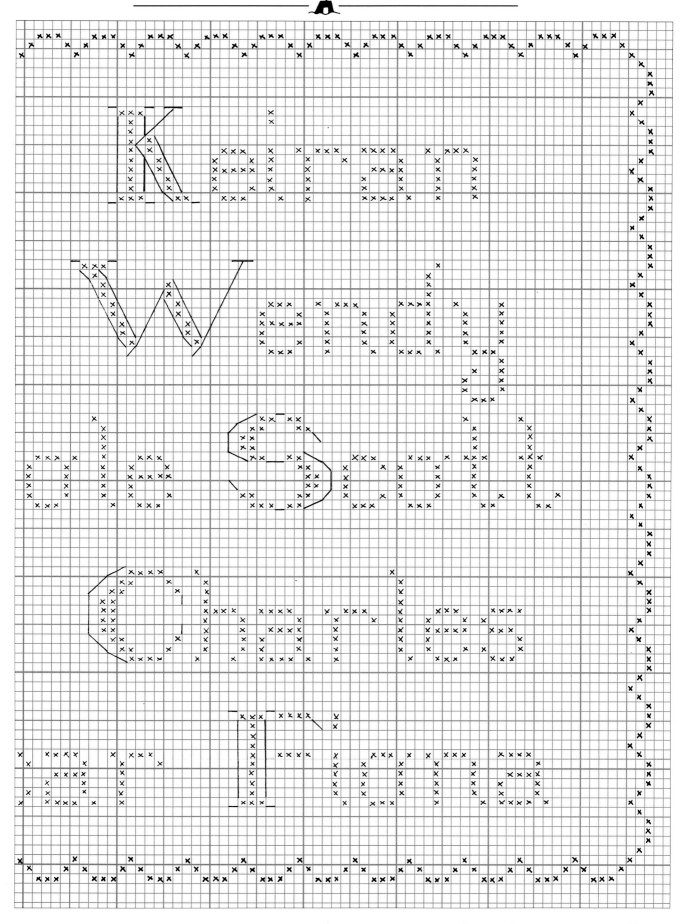

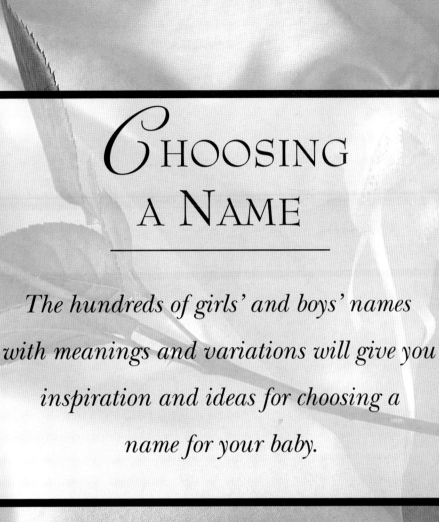

CHOOSING A NAME

*The hundreds of girls' and boys' names
with meanings and variations will give you
inspiration and ideas for choosing a
name for your baby.*

Girls' Names

ABIGAIL, (Hebrew) Father rejoiced.
Abigael; Abby; Abbey

ADA, (Teutonic) Noble.
Aida; Adela; Adele; Adila; Adelie; Edila; Adah; Ajda

ADELAIDE, (Teutonic) Noble and kind.
Adelaida; Adeline; Adelajda; Adeliza; Aline; Adalgisa

ADRIENNE, (Latin) From the Adriatic.
Adriana; Adrianna; Ariana; Ariane; Hadri

AGATHA, (Greek) Good.
Agathe; Agota; Agafia; Gytha; Aggie

AGNES, (Greek) Pure, chaste.
Agnesca; Agnese; Agnessa; Agnola; Anais; Anis; Annise; Ines; Inez; Nesta; Neza; Ynes; Agnessija; Agneta

AILEEN, (Irish from Greek) Light.

AINSLEY, (Old English) One's meadow.
Ainslea; Ainslee; Ainsly

ALANA, (Irish) 'O my child'.
Alannah; Alayna; Alaine

ALEXANDRA, (Greek) Defender of men.
Alessandra; Aleksandra; Alejandra; Alix; Lexine; Alexis; Alexa; Aleksia; Sasha; Alexandria

ALICE, (Teutonic) Noble.
Alissa; Alicia; Aleecia; Alisa; Alyce; Alys; Alyse

ALISON, (Teutonic) Son of the noble.
Allison; Allyson

ALMA, (Spanish) Soul.
Amber, (Egyptian) Light.

AMELIA, (Teutonic) Industrious.
Amalia; Amelie; Amelija; Amala

AMINAH, (Arabic) Honest, faithful.

AMY, (Old French) Lovable.
Aimee; Amie; Amity; Amorita

ANANSTASIE, (Greek) One who shall rise again.
Anastasia; Anastazja; Anastazya

ANDREA, (Greek) Womanly.
Andree; Andria

ANDRONICKY, (Greek) Victorious woman.

ANGELA, (Greek) Angel or messenger.
Angel; Angèle; Angelica; Angelika; Angeline; Angelique; Aniela; Anjela; Ancela

ANNE, (Hebrew) Graceful.
Ann; Anna; Annie; Anjuska; Annette; Annetta; Anka; Anica; Annike; Annis; Nan; Nanette; Vanka; Zaneta; Annusche

ANNABEL, (Hebrew) Graceful and beautiful.
Annabelle; Annabella

ANNELISE, (Hebrew) Graceful satisfaction.
Anneliese; Annalisa

ANTOINETTE, (Latin) Inestimable.
Antonia; Antonetta; Antonella; Antonya; Antoinetta

APRIL, AVRIL, The month.

ASTARTE, (Syrian) After the goddess of fertility in Syria.

ASTRID, ASTRIDE, (Old Norse) God's strength.

ATHENE, (Greek) After the goddess of wisdom.
Athena; Athenais; Athenaios

AUDREY, (Old English) Noble strength.
Aud; Audree; Audrie

AUGUSTYNA, (Latin) Venerable, sublime.
Augusta; Avgusta; Awsta; Agostinha; August; Agostina

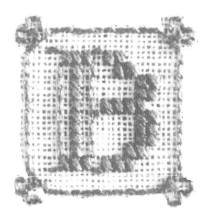

BARBARA, (Greek) Stranger or foreigner.
Babrischa; Barbary; Barbe; Barbule; Barbarina; Barbea; Barbica; Barbra; Barbro; Barbraa

BASIA, (Greek) Queenly.
Basila; Basillia

BEATRICE, (Latin) Bringer of joy.
Beatrix; Beatriz; Beatriks; Blazena

BELINDA, (Teutonic) Bringer of wisdom.

BENEDETTA, (Latin) Blessed.
Benedicta; Benedictina; Benedikta; Benita; Bettina

BERENICE, BERNICE, (Greek) Bringer of victory.

BERNADETTE, (Germanic) Stern bear.
Bernarda; Bernadetta; Bernadyna; Berneen

BERTHA, (Old English) Bright.
Berthe; Berta; Berthel; Bertilla; Bertle

BERYL, (Greek) Pure, after the jewel.

BETHANY, BETHEL, (Hebrew) House of God.

BETTY, Pet forms of Elizabeth — God is satisfied.
Bette; Beth; Beta; Bettje; Betsy; Bettys; Babette

BEVERLEY, (Old English) Beaver stream.
Beverly; Beverlee; Beverlie

BIANCA, BLANCHE, (Italian/French) White.

BILLIE, BILLEE, Diminutives of Wilhelmina — 'will' and 'resolve helmet'.

BONNY, BONNIE, (Scottish from French) Good and pretty.

BOZENA, BOZENKA, (Slavonic) God's favour.

BRENDA, (Norse) Sword.

BRIANA, (Irish) Hill.
Brianna; Brienna; Brina; Briony; Bryana

BRIDGET, (Celtic) The high one.
Brit; Briget; Brigitte; Brigyta; Brita; Brites; Berit; Brigida; Brighid

BRITTANY, A province of France.

BRONISLAVA, (Slavonic) Weapon glory.

BRONWYN, BRONWEN, (Welsh) White breast.

BROOKE, BROOK, (Old English) Of the brook.

BRUNA, (Italian from Teutonic) Brown.

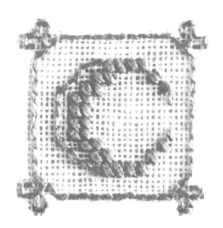

CAITLIN, (Gaelic) A form of Kathleen.

CAMILLA, (Etruscan) Attendant at a sacrifice.
Camille; Kamilla

CANDICE, CANDACE, (Greek) Fire white.

CARLA, Feminine of Charles — a man.

CARMEL, (Hebrew) The garden.

CARMEN, (Spanish from Hebrew) The garden.
Carmencita; Carmina; Carmelita; Carmela

CAROL, Diminutive of Caroline.
Carole; Carolle; Carroll; Karel; Karol

CAROLINE, Feminine of Charles — a man — through Carl.
Carolyn; Carline; Carlina; Carolina; Carolynn; Karolina; Charlene

CASIMIRA, (Slavonic) Peace proclaimed.

CASSANDRA, (Greek) After the prophetess of Troy.
Kassandra; Cassie

CATHERINE, (Greek) Pure.
Catharine; Caterina; Catana; Catriona

CECILIA, (Latin) Blind.
Celia; Cecily; Cacilie; Cecile; Cecylja; Cicely; Cecilya; Cecylia

CHANDRA, (Sanskrit) Charming, moon-like.

CHANTAL, (French) Singer.
Chantel; Chantelle

CHARIS, CHARISSA, (Greek) Grace.

CHARLOTTE, Feminine forms of Charles — a man.
Charlotta; Carlotta; Charlette; Cheryl

CHERIE, CHER, (French) Dear, beloved.

CHLOE, (Greek) Fresh green shoot.

CHRISTINA, (Latin) Christian.
Christine; Cristina; Cristine; Christinha; Kristen; Kristeen; Kristin; Kristyan; Kirstyn

CHRYZANTA, (Greek) Golden.
Chrysanthe; Chryseis

CLAIRE, (Latin) Bright, clear.
Clare; Clara; Chiara; Clareta; Clarissa; Klaara; Klara; Klarissa; Clair

CLAUDIA, (Latin) Lame.
Claudette; Claude; Clause; Klaudja; Claudine

COLETTE, COLETTA, French diminutive of Nicole.

COLLEEN, (Irish) Girl.

CONCHA, (Spanish) Shell.

CONSTANCE, (Latin) Constant.
Constancia; Constantina; Constanza; Gostanza; Konstancyna

CORINNE, (Greek) Coral.
Coral; Coralie

CRYSTAL, (Greek) Frost — after the gem.
Kristal; Krystal; Krystle

CYNTHIA, (Greek) A name for the moon-goddess.

DAISY, (English) Day's eye — the flower.

DALE, (Old English) Valley.

DANICA, (Slavonic) Morning star.

DANIELLE, (Hebrew) God is my judge.
Daniela; Danetta; Danila; Dannetej; Danya

DAPHNE, (Greek) Laurel — the flower.

DAWN, After the dawn of the day.
Aurora; Aurore

DEBORAH, (Hebrew) A bee.
Debra; Debbie

DEIDRE, DEIRDRE, (Gaelic) Sorrow.

DENISE, (Greek) After Dionysius, the god of wine.
Denice; Denyse; Dionyse; Dionysia; Zdena

DIANA, (Latin) After the moon goddess.
Diane; Deanne; Diahann; Dian; Dionne; Dyana; Dianne; Deanna; Dyan

DINAH, DYNA, (Hebrew) Vindicated.

DOBRANA, DOBRIJA, (Slavonic) Good.

DOLORES, (Spanish) Sorrow.
Delore; Dolor; Dolour; Delores

DOMINIQUE, (Latin) Follower of the Lord.
Dominica; Dominga; Dominika

DONNA, (Latin) Lady.

DOREEN, (Irish) A form of Dorothy — gift.

DORIS, (Greek) After the mother of the nymphs.

DOROTHY, (Greek) Gift of God.
Dorothée; Dora; Dorotea; Dorothea; Doretta; Dort; Dorothya; Dorothe

DRAGA, (Slavonic) Dear.
Dragana; Draganka; Draglika

DUSA, DUSCHA, (Slavonic) Happy.

EDITH, (Old English) Rich, happy and warlike.
Edit; Edita; Editha; Ediva; Edyth; Edytha; Edythe

EDNA, (Celtic) Ardent.

EDWINA, (Old English) Rich, happy, friendly.

EILEEN, EILENE, (Irish from Greek) Light.

ELAINE, (Old French from Greek) Light.
Elayne; Elana; Laine

ELEANOR, (Provencal from Greek) Light.
Eleanora; Aelinor; Elyenora; Lenor; Lenore; Alienor

ELENI, Forms of Helen — Light.
Ellen; Elene

ELIZABETH, (Hebrew) Satisfactory to God.
Elisabeth; Eliza; Elisabetta; Elisavetta; Elise; Elizabet; Elsa; Elsbeth; Elspeth; Elzbieta; Erihapeti; Erzbet; Lisbeth; Lisabeth; Liza; Lizabeth; Lizbeta; Lizette; Lisa; Elsbetchen; Betty; Bess; Libby; Elsie; Elzinha; Bets; Babette

ELLA, (Teutonic) All.

ELLE, (French) She.

EMILY, (Latin) Industrious.
Emilia; Emiliana; Emilie; Emeline; Emilija; Emiliya; Emmeline; Emmy

EMMA, (Teutonic) Whole, universal.
Ama; Hemma

EMMANUELLE, (Hebrew) God is with us.
Emanuela; Manuela

ENID, (Welsh) Spirit.

ERICA, ERIKA, (Teutonic) Ruler.

ERIN, Ancient poetic name for Ireland.
Erina; Eryn

ESTHER, (Persian) Star.
Hester; Eszter; Ester

ETHEL, (Old English) Noble.

EUGENIE, (Greek) Noble and excellent.
Eugenia; Yevgenia

EULALIA, (Greek) Sweetly speaking.
Eulalie; Eualija; Ulalai

EVA, (Hebrew) Lively.
Eve; Ewa; Ebba

EVELYN, From a place name near Coutances in Normandy.

FAITH, The virtue.
Fidelia; Fides

FARRAH, (Old English) Beautiful, pleasant.

FAUSTYNA, (Latin) Lucky.
Fausta; Faustina

FAY, A diminutive of Faith or Fairy.
Faye; Fae

FELICITY, (Latin) Happy.
Felicia; Felicidad; Felicissma; Feliciza; Felis; Felisia; Feliza; Phelissitie

FERNANDA, FERNANDE, (Teutonic)

Adventurous.

FIAMETTA, (Italian) Little flame.

FIONA, (Gaelic) Fair one.

FLEUR, Flower.
Flora; Flower

FLORENCE, (Latin) Blooming.
Florencia; Florencya; Florida

FRANCES, (Latin) Free.
Francesca; Francine; Fran; Francisca; Françoise; Franka; Frantisek; Franziska; Frasquita; Paquita

FREDA, (Teutonic) Peaceful ruler.
Frieda; Frederica; Frydryka; Fritzi; Fredrica

FREYA, (Old Norse) Goddess of love and beauty.

GERDA, (Teutonic) Guarded.

GINA, GEENA, Diminutive for Angelina, Regina, etc.

GISELLA, (Teutonic) Pledge.
Giselle; Gizelle; Ghislaine

GLADYS, GWLADYS, Welsh form of Claudia — lame.

GLENDA, (Welsh) Valley.
Glennis; Glenice; Glynnis

GLORIA, (Latin) Glory.

GRACE, (Latin) Grace.
Grazia; Engracia; Graciela

GRETA, Diminutive of Margaret — pearl.

GWENDOLEN, (Welsh) white or white browed.
Gwendolyn; Gwendoline; Gwenda; Gwen

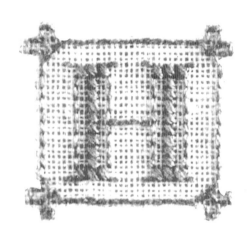

GABRIELLE, (Hebrew) Feminine form of the name of the Angel of the Annunciation.
Gabriella; Gabriela; Gabryela; Gabrilla; Gabella

GAIL, GAYLE, (Hebrew) Rejoice.

GALINA, Russian form of Helen — light.

GEMMA, JEMMA, (Latin) Gem.

GENEVIEVE, (Celtic) White wave.
Genofeva; Genovera; Genowica; Jenofeva

GEORGIA, (Greek) Feminine of George — farmer.
Georgina; Georgiana; Georgette; Georgianna; Gjurgjinka

GERALDINE, (Teutonic) Spear rule.
Geralda; Gerhardine; Giralda

HABIBAH, (Arabic) Beloved.

HANNAH, (Hebrew) Grace.
Hana; Hanna

HANNELORE, German linking of Jane and Laura.

HARRIET, Derived from Harry — ruler of the house.
Hariette; Harried

HAYLEY, HAYLEE, (Old English) High clearing.

HAZEL, (Old English) Hazel tree.

HEATHER, After the plant.

HEDWIG, (Teutonic) War refuge.
Hedy; Hedviga; Hedwegis; Jadwiga

HEIDI, Diminutive of Adelaide or Hedwig.

HELEN, (Greek) Light.
Helena; Galina; Hélène; Helenka; Ileana; Ilona; Ellen; Eleni; Ellie

HENRIETTA, (Teutonic) Ruler of the house.
Henriette; Hendrica; Henrieta; Henryka; Jendriska; Jindriska

HILARY, (Greek) Cheerful, merry.

HILDA, (Teutonic) Battle, war maiden.
Hilde; Hylda

HOLLY, HOLLIE, After the plant.

HONG, (Chinese) Pink.

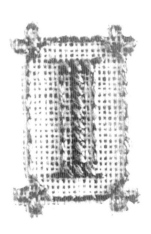

IDA, (Norse) Labour or (Teutonic) Divine.

IGNACYA, (Latin) Ardent, fiery.
Ignacia; Ignazia; Ignatia

IMOGEN, IMOGENE, (Irish) Daughter.

INEZ, INES, Spanish and Portugese forms of Agnes — pure.

INGA, (Old Norse) After the old Norse god Ingvi or Ingvi's ride.
Ingrid; Inge

IRENE, (Greek) Peace.
Irena; Eereena; Irina

IRIS, (Greek) Rainbow.

ISABELLE, Forms of Elizabeth — God is satisfied, incorporating Bella — beautiful.
Isabel; Isabella; Isobel; Isbel; Ysabel; Izabel; Isabelhina

IVANA, Forms of Joanna — Jehovah has favoured.
Ivanna; Ivanku

IVY, The clinging vine.

JACINTA, (Greek) Hyacinth.
Jacinth; Jacintha; Hyacintha

JACOBA, Feminine of Jacob — supplanter.
Jacobina; Jakuba; Jacobella

JACQUELINE, Feminine form of James — supplanter.
Jaclyn; Jaclynn; Jacquetta; Jackie

JADE, (Spanish) The precious stone.

JANE, (Hebrew) Jehovah has favoured.
Hanne; Janet; Janis; Janice; Jayne; Janina; Janetta; Vanya; Janette; Heni; Janelle; Janine

JAROSLAVA, JAROSLAVNA, (Slavonic) Spring glory.

JASMIN, (Persian) The flower.
Jasmine; Yasmin

JEAN, (Hebrew) Jehovah has favoured.
Jeanette; Jeanne; Jeanine; Janella; Jeannie

JENNIFER, (Celtic) White wave.
Ginevra; Jennavah; Jennifah; Jenufa

JESSICA, (Hebrew) He beholds.
Jesseka; Jessika; Jessie; Jess; Jessye

JILL, English forms of Juliana — Roman family name — soft hair.
Jillian; Gill; Gillian; Jillie; Jilly; Jillianne

JOANNA, (Hebrew) Jehovah has favoured.
Joanne; Johanna; Joan; Jone; Joni; Jovanna; Jovka

JOCELYN, JOCELIN, (Latin) Merry.

JODIE, JODY, (Hebrew) From Judah.

JORDAN, (Hebrew) Flowing down.

JOSEPHINE, (Hebrew) Jehovah added.
Josefa; Josefina; Josephe; Josette; Jozefa

JOY, (Old French from Latin) Vivid pleasure.

JOYCE, JOYCIA, (Celtic) After a French saint.

JUANITA, JUANA, Spanish forms of Joanna — Jehovah has favoured.

JUDITH, (Hebrew) From Judah.
Jude; Judah; Judit; Judithe; Judy; Dita; Juczi

JULIA, Roman family name. Soft hair.
Julie; Juliet; Julietta; Juliana; Guilette; Julya; Julienne; Julianja; Julis; Julka; Yulia

JUNE, From Juno, the wife of Jupiter — the name of the month.

JUSTINE, (Latin) Just.
Justina; Justa; Justilla; Giusta; Giustina

KAREN, Forms of Katherine — pure.
Caren; Carin; Karina; Karyn

KATE, Diminutive of Katherine.

KATHERINE, (Greek) Pure.
Katharine; Catherine; Kathleen; Kathryn; Katie;

Kaitlyn; Carin; Cathryn; Kathryn; Kate; Kari; Kasia; Katalin; Kateriny; Kathri; Katia; Katina; Katrijin; Katrina; Katya; Kay; Kaye; Kit; Kitty; Trina; Kasche; Catriona; Caitlin; Catlin; Catalina; Caterina; Kato; Cathie; Cathy

KATHLEEN, Irish form of Katherine.

KAYE, KAY, (Greek) Rejoicing or diminutive of Katherine.

KELLY, (Irish) Descendant of war.

KERRY, KERRIE, (Celtic) Dark.

KHADIJA, (Arabic) After a wife of Muhammad.

KIM, KIMBERLEY, (Old English) Chief or royal place.

KIRSTY, KIRSTIE, Scottish pet names for Christine.

KRISTEN, Forms of Christine.
Kristijntje; Kristin; Kristy

KYLIE, (Aboriginal) Boomerang.

LARA, (Latin) The shining one.

LARISSA, (Greek) Cheerful.

LATEEFA, LATIFA, (Arabic) Gentle, pleasant.

LAURA, (Latin) Bay tree.
Lauren; Laurel; Laurentia; Laurette; Loren; Lorene; Lorenja; Lorenza; Loretta; Lorette; Laure

LEA, (Latin) Lioness.

LEAH, (Hebrew) Cow.

LEANNE, LEIGHANNE, Lee + Anne.

LEE, (Old English) Meadow or Chinese surname.

LEIGH, (Old English) Meadow.

LEONIDA, (Latin) Lion-like.
Leonie; Leona; Leon; Leone; Leonice; Leontine; Leontyne

LEONORA, Forms of Helen — light.
Leonore; Lenore

LESLEY, LESLIE, Scottish place name.

LILIAN, Pet forms of Elizabeth.
Lillian; Lila; Liliane; Lilliane

LILY, After the flower.
Lili; Lilly

LINDA, (Teutonic) Wise.
Lynda; Lindy

LISA, LIZA, Pet forms of Elizabeth.

LOIS, (Greek) Loosened, freed.

LOLA, Diminutive of Dolores.

LORNA, (Celtic) After a moor goddess.

LORRAINE, LARAINE, (Teutonic) After the old duchy in France.

LOUISE, (Teutonic) Listener.
Louisa; Luisa; Ludwika; Luise; Elouise; Eloise; Luiza; Luizinha

LUCY, (Latin) Light.
Lucia; Luciana; Lucie; Lucille; Lucina; Lucinda; Lucka; Lucya; Luzie; Luz

LYN, (Celtic) Pool.
Lynn; Lynne; Lynette

MADELEINE, (Hebrew) Woman of Magdala, after St. Mary Magdalen.
Madeline; Madelon; Magdalen; Madalena; Madalene; Marlene; Magdala; Magdalena; Magdolna; Magna; Maddy

MARCIA, (Latin) Of the god Mars.
Marcea; Marcelle; Marcellina; Marsha; Marcie

MARGARET, (Latin from Greek) Pearl.
Marguerite; Malgerita; Margo; Margot; Margrethe; Margriet; Marjory; Mairead; Mairgret; Greta; Gretel; Madge; Maharite; Margaux; Margery; Marjarita; Marketa; Markete; Maida; Gretel; Madlinka; Maggie; Maije; Malgosia; Margarete; Margit; Margryta; Mairead; Rita

MARIA, Latin forms of Mary.
Mariah; Marea

MARILYN, Mary + Lyn.

MARINA, MARINHA, (Latin) Of the sea.

MARION, Of Mary.
Marian; Mariana; Marianne

MARLENE, Mary + Magdalene.

MARTHA, (Aramaic) Lord.
Marta; Marthe; Maata

MARTINA, MARTINE, (Latin) Of Mars, the war god.

MARY, (Hebrew) Bitterly wanted child.
Maria; Marie; Maree; Maritsa; Mariamne; Maryke; Molly; Manon; Mariette; Marietta; Marita; Marya; Marynia; Marysia; Manette; Markika; Marjanka

MAUD, (Teutonic) Battle strife.
Maude; Maudie

MAUREEN, MAURINE, Irish form of Mary.

MAVIS, (English) Thrush.

MAXINE, MAXIMA, (Latin) The greatest.

MAY, MAE, Diminutives of Mary or from the flower or month.

MEGAN, Welsh forms of Margaret — pearl.
Meagan; Meaghan; Meghan; Meghann

MELANIE, (Greek) Black.
Melania; Melony

MELINA, (Greek) Gentle.

MELINDA, Melanie + Linda.

MELISSA, (Greek) Honey or sweet.
Melesa; Melisse; Millice

MEREDITH, (Welsh) Lord from the sea.

MERLE, MERYL, Of the sea or blackbird.

MICAELA, Feminine form of Michael — who is like the Lord?
Michelle; Miguela; Mikaela; Mikala; Miquela; Micala; Michaela

MILA, (Slavonic) Lovable.
Milana; Milo

MILKA, (Slavonic) Industrious.

MIRANDA, (Latin) Worthy to be admired.

MIRIAM, (Hebrew) Bitter or bitterly wanted.
Mariamne; Miriamme

MITZI, German form of Maria.

MOIRA, Irish form of Mary.

MOLLY, Diminutive of Mary.

MONA, (Irish) Noble.
Moina; Moya

MONICA, (African) Alone.
Monique; Monika; Monike; Monette

MORGAN, (Celtic) Sea bright.
Morgana; Morgaine

MYFANWY, (Welsh from Hebrew) Pleasant.
Myffany; Myfina

MYRA, MIRA, (Greek from Hebrew) Flowing.

NADA, (Slovak) Hope.
Nadine; Nadezda; Nadedjda; Nadia; Nadan

NANCY, Pet names of Anne — grace.
Nan; Nana; Nanette

NAOMI, (Hebrew) Pleasant.

NARELLE, (Aboriginal) Place.

NATALIE, (Latin) Christmas Day.
Natalia; Natalee; Natasha; Nathalie; Natale

NELL, Pet forms of Eleanor or Helen.
Nellie; Nelly

NERIDA, NERIDAH, (Aboriginal) Blossom.

NICOLA, (Greek) Victorious.
Nicole; Nicolette; Nicolle

NOELINE, (Latin) Christmas.
Noeleen; Noelle; Noella

NORMA, (Latin) Rule, pattern.

PENELOPE, (Greek) Bobbin.
Penolpa; Penny

PETA, (Greek from Aramaic) Rock.
Petronilla; Peronne; Petra; Petronelle; Petrisse; Petrija; Petronhila

PHILIPPA, (Greek) Lover of horses.
Phillipa; Filippa; Filipa; Felipa; Pip; Pippa

PHOEBE, (Greek) Shining one.
Febe; Feebee; Phebe; Feba

PHYLLIS, (Greek) Leafy.
Phillis; Filis

PIA, (Latin) Devout.

PILAR, (Spanish from Latin) Pillar, meaning strong and tall.

POLLY, Rhymes with Molly. Pet name for Mary.

PRISCILLA, (Latin) Former.
Prisca; Preziosilla; Priscille

OLGA, (Norse) Holy.
Helga; Olva; Olenka

OLIVIA, (Latin) Olive.
Olive; Livia

PALOMA, (Spanish) Dove.

PAMELA, (English) Invented in 1590.
Pamella; Pamina

PATRICIA, (Latin) Noble.
Patrice; Patreeza; Patrizia; Patrycyka; Pat; Patty; Tricia

PAULA, (Latin) Small.
Pauline; Paulette; Paulisca; Pavia; Pavlica; Paola; Paule

PEARL, (Latin) Pearl.
Pearla; Perla

RACHEL, (Hebrew) Ewe.
Rachael; Rachela; Raquel; Rahel

RAMONA, (Teutonic) Mighty protector.
Ramonda; Raymunda; Rae; Raema

REBECCA, (Hebrew) Heifer.
Reba; Rebekah; Rebeccah; Rebeka

RENEE, RENE, (Latin) Born Again.

RHIANNON, RHIANNE, (Welsh) Nymph.

ROBERTA, (Teutonic) Bright fame.
Robertha; Robetta

ROBYN, Diminutive of Roberta.
Robin; Robina

ROSALIE, (Latin) From rosalia, the ceremony of hanging roses in tombs.
Rosalia; Rosalija; Rosel; Rozalie; Rozalja; Ruzalia

ROSALIND, (Teutonic) Horse serpent.
Rosalinda; Rosalynda; Roslyn; Rozalyn

ROSAMUND, (Teutonic) Horse protection.
Rosamund; Rosemunda; Rozamond

ROSE, The flower.
Rosa; Rhoda; Rosetta; Roza; Rozina; Ruusu; Ruzena

ROSEMARY, The herb.
Rosemarie; Rosemarin

ROWENA, (Saxon) Famous friend.

ROXANA, (Persian) Dawn.
Roxanne; Roxane

RUTH, (Hebrew) Kind.
Rute; Ruthe; Ruthina; Ruut

SALIDA, (Arabic) Happy.
Zelida; Selde

SALLY, Diminutive of Sarah.

SALOME, (Aramaic) Peace of Zion.
Salaome; Salomee; Salomea; Saloma

SAMANTHA, (Aramaic) Listener.

SANCHA, (Spanish) Holy.
Sancta; Sanctussa; Sanctuzza; Sancya; Santuzza; Sanchia

SANDRA, SANDRINE, Diminutive of Alexandra.

SARAH, (Hebrew) Princess.
Sara; Sari; Zara; Sarita; Shari; Sorcha; Zahra; Zarah; Saara; Sadie; Sally

SAVITRI, (Sanskrit) Inciter.

SELENA, (Greek) Moon.
Selina; Celina; Selene; Zelina

SHANNON, A river in Ireland.

SHARON, (Hebrew) Even, level plain.
Sharni; Sharolyn; Sharron

SHEILA, Irish form of Cecilia.

SHIRLEY, (Old English) Bright wood or clearing.
Shirlee; Sherley

SIBYL, (Greek from Latin) Wise woman.
Sibylla; Sibella; Sibila; Sibylle; Sybil; Cybille; Cybill; Cybil; Sybylla

SIMONE, (Hebrew) Listening.
Simonetta; Zimenia

SINEAD, An Irish form of Jane.

SIOBHAN, Irish form of Joanna.
Shivawn; Siobhain

SKYE, The largest island of the Inner Hebrides off Scotland.

SONIA, Sonja, Forms of Sophia — wise.

SOPHIE, (Greek) Wisdom.
Sophia; Sapienta; Sappe; Sonia; Sonja; Sophy; Zofia; Zosia; Zsofia

STELLA, (Latin) Star.
Estella; Estrelita; Estelle

STEPHANIE, (Greek) Crown.
Stéphane; Stephanida; Stepania; Estaphania; Etienette; Stefa; Stefanie; Stephanine; Stesha; Stevana; Stephany

SUSAN, (Hebrew) Lily.
Susanna; Suzanne; Susane; Susette; Suzette; Zosa; Zusanne; Zuzanna; Zozel; Zsa Zsa; Sue; Susie; Suzan

SYLVIA, (Latin) From the woods.
Silvia; Silvana; Sylwyn; Silvie

TAMARA, (Slavonic from Hebrew) Palm tree.

TANYA, After St. Tatiana.
Tania; Tanee; Tanja; Tatiana

TARA, (Irish) Hill or Saviour Goddess of Buddhist religion.

TERESA, (Greek) Reaper.
Terese; Thérèse; Tereza; Terezia; Theresa; Terza; Terezija; Teresina; Teresita; Terri; Terry; Terezie; Terezyga

TESS, TESSA, Contractions of Teresa.

THEA, (Greek) Divine.

THELMA, A contraction of Anthelma from Anselma (Greek) Divine helmut.

TIFFANY, (Greek) Born at Epiphany.
Tifaine; Epifania; Epiphanie; Tifanee; Tiffanie; Theophanie

TINA, Pet name for Christina, Bettina etc.

TRACY, TRACEY A modern form of Teresa.

URSULA, (Latin) Bear.
Ursa; Orsola; Orsolija; Urszula

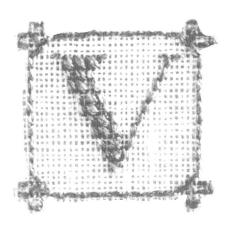

VALDA, (Norse) Battle.
Valma; Valmai

VALERIE, (Latin) Healthy.
Valeria; Valéry; Valeska; Waleria

VANESSA, Invented by Swift.

VERA, VJERA, (Russian) Faith.

VERONICA, (Latin) True image.
Veronike; Veroniky; Véronique; Phrenike

VICTORIA, (Latin) Victorious.
Victoire; Viktoria; Viktorija; Vittoria; Victorine; Vikki

VIOLET, The flower.
Violette; Viola; Violetta; Yolande; Yolanda; Jolande; Violante

VIRGINIA, VIRGINIE, (Latin) Virginal.

VIVIAN, (Latin) Alive, vital.
Vivien; Vivienne; Viviana

VLASTA, (Slavonic) Ruler.

YVONNE, (French) From the yew tree.
Yvette; Evonne

WANDA, (Teutonic) Stem.
Vanda; Wandis

WENDY, Invented by J. M. Barrie — Frendy
Wendy.

WILHELMINA, (Teutonic) 'Will' and 'resolve
helmet'.
*Guglielma; Guillema; Helmina; Wilma; Hilma;
Velma; Vilma; Willa; Vilhelmine*

WINIFRED, (Welsh) After a Welsh princess.
*Winfred; Wynifreed; Winnifred; Win; Winnie;
Gwenfrewi; Wenfreda*

ZARA, ZAHRA, Arabic forms of Sarah.

ZOE, (Greek) Life.
Ziva; Zoia; Zivka

BOYS' NAMES

AARON, (Egyptian) The exalted or enlightened one.

ABRAHAM, (Hebrew) Father of the multitude.
Abe; Abram; Ibrahim; Avraam; Abrahan

ADAM, (Hebrew) Red.

ADRIAN, (Latin) From the Adriatic region.
Adriano; Adriaan; Hadrien

AIDAN, (Irish) Fire.

ALAN, (Celtic) Noble, cheerful.
Allan; Allen; Alain

ALASTAIR, (Gaelic from Greek) Defender of men.
Alaster; Alistair; Alasdair

ALBERT, ALBERTO, (Old German) Noble.

ALDO, (Italian from German) Old.

ALEXANDER, (Greek) Defender of men.
Alejandro; Alexandre; Alex; Alec; Alexis; Alejo; Aleksander; Aleksandr; Aleksy; Sandor; Sasha; Sacha; Lex; Alezios; Aleizo

ALI, (Arabic) The exalted one.

AMIN, (Arabic) Trustworthy.

ANATOL, ANATOLE, (Greek) Rising from the east like the sun.

ANDREW, (Greek) Manly.
Andras; Andreas; André; Anders; Andrei; Andrea

ANGELO, (Italian from Greek) Angel.
Angelico; Angiolo

ANGUS, (Gaelic) Vigorous choice.

ANTHONY, (Latin) Flourishing.
Antony; Antonio; Antal; Antoine; Antonin; Anton; Tony; Tonio

ARNOLD, (Old German) Eagle power.
Arnoldo; Arend; Arnoldas

ARTHUR, (Celtic) Bear.
Artur; Arturo; Artor; Artorioos

ASHLEY, ASHLIE, (Old English) Dweller in the ashtree meadow.

BARRY, BARRIE, (Irish) Spear.

BART, (Hebrew) Plough-man.
Bartholomew; Bartek; Bartholomeo; Barteo

BASILIO, (Greek) Kingly.
Basil; Vassili; Vassily

BENEDICT, (Latin) Blessed.
Benedetto; Beniamino; Benito; Bengt; Benedicto

BENJAMIN, (Hebrew) Son of the right hand.
Beniamino; Binyamin

BERNARD, (Old German) Stern bear.
Bernardo; Bernhard; Berents; Bernaldo

BLAIR, (Irish) From the marshy plain.

BLAKE, (Old English) Black, dark.

BRAD, BRADLEY, (Old English) From the broad meadow.

BRANDON, BRANDEN, (Irish) Raven.

BRENDAN, BRENDON, (Old Irish) Sword.

BRIAN, (Old Irish) Hill.
Brien; Bryan

BRUCE, (French/Gaelic) Originally from a place in France.

BRUNO, BRUNON, (Old German) Brown.

CRAIG, (Scots) Crag.

CYRIL, (Greek) Lord.
Cyrille; Cirillo; Kyril; Cyryl; Ciril

CALLUM, CALUM, (Gaelic) Devotee of St. Columb.

CAMERON, (Gaelic) Crooked nose.

CAMPBELL, (Gaelic) Crooked mouth.

CASIMIR, (Polish) Peach proclaimed.
Casimira; Kasimir; Kazimierz

CHARLES, (Teutonic) A man.
Karl; Carl; Carol; Carlos; Karoly; Karel; Carlo; Charlie

CHRISTIAN, (Latin) A Christian.
Christos; Chrystjan; Kristian; Christo; Krischan; Hristoslav; Karstin

CHRISTOPHER, (Greek) Bearer of Christ.
Christof; Christophe; Chris; Kristopher; Kit; Christophoro; Christovac; Krzysztof

CLAUDE, (Latin) Lame.
Claudio; Claudius; Klaud; Klavdi

CLEMENT, (Latin) Mild, merciful.
Clemence; Clemens; Clemente; Clemento; Klement

CLIFFORD, CLIFF, (Old English) Ford at the cliff.

CLIVE, (Old English) At the cliff.

COLIN, COLAN, (From Greek) Peaceful.

CONNOR, CONOR, (Irish) High will.

CONRAD, (Old German) Bold council.
Conrado; Curt; Konrad; Coen; Coenraad; Cort

CONSTANTINE, (Latin) Steadfast, firm.
Con; Constantin; Constantinos; Konstantin; Kostya; Kostadin; Constantio; Kostusia; Kotka

CORNELIUS, (Latin) A horn.
Cornelis; Cornelio; Kornelius; Kees; Korneliusz

DAMIAN, (Greek) To tame.
Damien; Damiano; Damiao; Damionos

DANIEL, (Hebrew) God has judged.
Daneel; Danelo; Daniele; Danilo; Taniel

DARREN, (Greek) A Dorian.
Daren; Darrin; Daron; Dorian

DARYL, (French) Beloved.
Darrell; Darryll

DAVID, (Hebrew) Darling, beloved.

DEAN, DEANE, (Old English) Of the valley.

DECLAN, (Irish) After a saint.
Decklan; Deklan

DEMETRIOS, (Greek) Sacred to Demeter, the corn goddess.
Demetri; Dimiter; Dimitris; Dimitry; Dmitri

DENIS, (Greek) Follower of Dionysos, the god of wine.
Dennis; Denys; Dion; Dionigio; Dionis; Dionisio; Dionizy; Tents; Zbigniew

DEREK, DERRICK, (Greek) People's ruler.

DICK, RICK, Diminutives of Richard.

DIETRICH, (Greek) People's ruler.
Didrick; Dischis; Diedrik; Dierk; Dirk

DOMINIC, (Latin) Follower of the Lord.
Domenico; Domenikos; Domingo; Dominik; Dominique; Domokos

DONALD, DONAL, (Celtic) World and mighty.

DOUGLAS, (Gaelic) Dark blue.
Duglas; Douglass

DUNCAN, (Old Irish) Brown warrior.

DYLAN, (Celtic) Son of the wave.
Dilan; Dillon

EDGAR, (Old English) Rich and happy.
Edgardo; Edgard

EDMUND, (Old English) Rich, happy, protected.
Edmond; Edmundo; Edmondo; Eamon; Eamonn

EDWARD, (Old English) Rich, happy, guarded.
Eduardo; Edvard; Eduard; Edvardus

EDWIN, (Old English) Happy, rich friend.
Eduino; Edvinas; Ouen

ELIAS, (Hebrew) Jehovah is God.
Elia; Elija; Elijas; Ellis; Ilya

EMIL, (Latin) Industrious.
Emilio; Emile; Aemilius; Emlyn

ERIC, (Old German) Ever king.
Eirik; Erich; Erik; Eryk

ERNEST, (Old German) Earnest vigour.
Ernesto; Erneste; Ernestus; Ernst; Hernais

ERROL, (Old English) Nobleman.
Earl; Earle

EUGENE, (Greek) Well born.
Eugenes; Eugenio; Eugenius; Ewen; Yugany

EVAN, (Welsh) Jehovah has favoured.

EVERARD, (Old German) Boar hardy.
Everhard; Eberardo; Eberhart; Ebilo; Everett; Ewart

FADIL, (Arabic) Generous.

FAROUK, (Arabic) One who knows right from wrong.
Faroukh; Farruccio

FELIX, (Latin) Happy.
Felice; Feliciano; Feliks

FERDINAND, (Old German) Adventurous life.
Ferdinando; Fernando; Ferrand; Ferrante

FRANCIS, (Latin) Free.
Francisco; Francesco; Franc; Ferencz; Francisek; Franju; Frank; Frantik; Franz; Wherahiko; François

FREDERICK, (Teutonic, Old German) Peaceful ruler.
Bedric; Bedrich; Federico; Frederico; Frederik; Fridrich

FULKO, (Teutonic) Of the people.
Fulk; Fulke; Foke; Fokker; Folker; Fowke; Volker

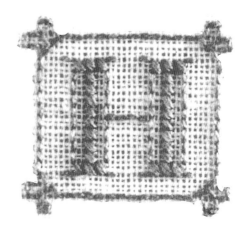

GABRIEL, (Hebrew) Strong man of God.
Gabriello; Jibri; Gabor; Gabrieius; Gavril

GARY, (Welsh) Old Man.
Gareth; Gerontius

GEOFFREY, (Teutonic) Man of peace.
Geofredo; Jeffery; Jeffrey; Goffredo; Gioffredo

GEORGE, (Greek) Farmer.
Georgio; Georgios; Jurgen; Jorge; Jurgis; Jurica; Gheorghe; Georges; Egor; Djoro; Geordie; Georgius

GERARD, (Teutonic) Spear ruler.
Gerald; Garcia; Garratt; Gerrit; Giraldo; Jerrold; Gerd; Gert; Gerardus; Gebhard; Gerardo

GILBERT, (Teutonic) Bright pledge.
Gilberto; Gisbert; Giselbert; Gysbert

GLEN, (Gaelic) Valley.
Glenn; Glyn; Glynn

GOFREDO, (Old German) God's peace.
Godfrey; Goffredo; Gottfried; Gotfryd

GORDON, (Gaelic) Great hill.

GRAEME, (Old English) Gravelly homestead.
Graham; Grahame

GRANT, (Old English) Big, tall.

GREGORY, (Greek) Watchful.
Gregor; Gregorie; Gregorio; Gregorijie; Grégoire; Grigory

GRIFFITH, GRIFFIN, (Welsh) Strong lord.

GUIDO, (Teutonic) Wide.
Guy; Wido

HABIB, (Arabic) Beloved.

HAMISH, (Gaelic from Hebrew) Supplanter.

HARI, (Sanskrit) He who removed sin. One of the names of Krishna.

HAROLD, (Old Norse) Army power.
Haraldo; Haroldas; Harald

HENRY, (Teutonic) House ruler.
Harry; Harrison; Enrico; Enrikas; Enrique; Enriquo; Ensilo; Enzio; Hein; Jindrich; Heine; Heintje; Hal; Heinrich; Heinz; Henare; Hendrik; Henri; Henryk

HERMAN, (Teutonic) Warrior.
Hermann; Ermanno; Ermas; Hermando; Hermon; Hermano; Hermanus

HO, (Chinese) River.

HOWARD, (Teutonic) Brave, hardy.

HUGH, (Teutonic) Heart and mind.
Hugo; Hues; Hugues; Huig; Huw; Hew

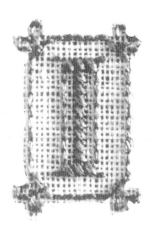

IAN, (Scottish form of John) Jehovah has favoured.
Iain; Ion; Ean

IGNACE, (Greek) Fire.
Ignacy; Ignatius; Ignasha; Inigo; Ignazio

IGOR, IGNMAR, (Old Norse) Famous son.

ISAAC, (Hebrew) God will smile upon me.
Isaak; Izak; Yitzhak

ISADOR,
(Greek) Gift from Isis, goddess of Egypt.

Idadore; Isidor; Isidoro; Eesidor

IVAN, forms of John.
Ivon; Yvann

JACK, A diminutive of John (Hebrew) God has favoured.

JACOB, (Hebrew) Supplanter.
Jacques; Jaak; Jacobo; Yaakov

JAMES, (Hebrew) Supplanter.
Jamie; Diego; Giocomo; Hamish; Seamus; Tascja; Jeka; Jasderika; Jim

JARED, (Greek) Rose.
Jarod; Jarrod

JASON, (Greek from Hebrew) Healer.

JEREMY, (Greek) Sacred name.
Jerone; Geronimo; Hieronymus; Jerko; Hieronomo; Jeremiah; Jeriamjasz; Jeromino

JESSE, (Hebrew) Jehovah is.

JOEL, (Hebrew) Jehovah is God.

JOHN, (Hebrew) Jehovah has favoured (us).
Jan; Jean; Jenick; Jens; Joannoelos; Jehan; Joh; Jack; Giankos; Ivan; Johan; Johannes; Sean; Juan; Shane; Evan; Jussi; Yiannis; Jock; Jackson; Hone; Jannes; Janek; Janos

JONATHAN, (Hebrew) Jehovah has given us a son.
Jonathon; Johnathan; Jon

JORDAN, JORDANES, (Hebrew) Flowing down.

JOSEPH, (Hebrew) Jehovah has added a child.
Jose; Giuseppe; Jorgen; Josef; Josip; Jusuf; Yusuf; Joe; Jozef; Joska; Jozsef; Josif

JOSHUA, YASSER, (Hebrew) Jehovah is my help.

JULIAN, (Latin) Of the Julian family.
Jules; Guiliano; Jolyon; Julien; Juliao; Julio

JUSTIN, (Latin) Just.
Justinian; Giustino; Iusto; Justo; Justino; Yestin; Justyn

KALID, KAHLID, (Arabic) Eternal.

KEITH, (Scottish) A place name.

KELVIN, (Celtic) From the narrow river.

KEMAL, (Turkish) Perfection.

KENNETH, (Gaelic) Comely.

KEVIN, (Irish) Comely.

KHALIF, (Arabic) Friend.

KIERAN, (Irish) Dark man.
Keeran; Keiran; Kier

KIRK, (Old Norse) Church.

KRISHNA, (Sanskrit) Black.

KYLE, (Gaelic) Scottish place name.

LACHLAN, (Gaelic) Man from the lake land.
Lochlan; Loughlin

LADISLAUS, (Slavonic) Power and glory.
Ladislav; Ladislas; Lako; Wladislav

LANCE, (Teutonic) Servant of the land.
Lancelot; Lanzo

LAURENCE, (Latin) Crowned by laurels.
Lawrence; Lars; Lorenzo; Laurent; Loris; Lauro; Laurie; Laurans

LEE, LEIGH, (Old English) Meadow or Chinese name.

LEO, (Latin) Lion-like.
Leon; Lav; Lev; Leos

LEONARD, (Germanic) Brave like a lion.
Leonardo; Lennart; Leonid; Leen

LESLIE, (Gaelic) Garden by the pool.

LIAM, Irish form of William.

LINDSAY, LINDSEY, (Old English) Lelli's Island.

LEWELLYN, (Welsh) Leader of lions.
Llewelyn; Lewelen

LLOYD, (Welsh) Grey.
Loyd; Floyd

LOUIS, (Germanic) To hear.
Lewis; Lajos; Ludovico; Ludvig; Ludwig; Luigi; Luis; Lodoe; Luiz; Rewi; Lodovico

LUCIANO, (Latin) Of light.
Lucian; Lucien

LUKE, (Latin) Light.
Lucas; Luka; Lukas; Lukasz; Luc

MOSES, (Egyptian) Child.
Moshe; Moss; Moyse; Mojzesz

MUHAMMAD, (Arabic) Praised.
Mohammed; Mumid

MURRAY, (Gaelic) A seaboard settlement.

MALCOLM, (Gaelic) Servant of St. Colomb.

MALIK, (Arabic) Possessor.

MANFRED, MANFREDO, (Germanic) Man of peace.

MARIO, (Latin) Of the war god Mars.
Marius; Mariusz

MARK, (Latin) Of Mars, the god of war.
Marcus; Marc; Marcos; Marco; Marek; Markku

MARTIN, (Latin) Of Mars, the god of war.
Maarten; Martijn; Martyn; Martinho; Martinus

MATTHEW, (Hebrew) Gift of God.
Mathew; Matthieu; Mathias; Matthias; Mat; Mats; Mate; Macisk; Macias; Matui; Mattea

MAURICE, (Latin) A dark man.
Maurizio; Mauricio; Mauri; Marits; Moreno; Morris

MAX, (Latin) A combination of two Roman family names.
Maximilian; Maximilien; Maxim; Maximo; Massimo

MICHAEL, (Hebrew) Who is like the Lord?
Michel; Michele; Miguel; Mischa; Mikko; Mikhail; Mihael; Mischa; Mickey

MILAN, (Slavonic) Loveable.

MILES, (Germanic) Mild, merciful.
Myles; Milo

MINOS, (Greek) Traditional name of the kings of Crete.

MITCHELL, (Old English) Big or a form of Michael.

MORGAN, (Celtic) Sea bright.

NATHAN, NATHAM, (Hebrew) Gift.

NATHANIEL, (Hebrew) God has given.
Nataniel; Nataniello; Nafanael

NEIL, (Irish) Champion.
Neal; Neel; Nial; Njal

NELSON, (Old English) Son of Nell.

NEVILLE, (Old French) New town.

NICHOLAS, (Greek) Victory of the people.
Nicolas; Claus; Klaas; Nicol; Nicolo; Nicodomenus; Miklos; Colas; Nicodeme; Nicolaio; Nikodem; Niklaus; Nick; Nikola; Nikolai

NINO, NINIAN, (Italian) The name of a saint.

NOEL, (Old French from Latin) Christmas.
Natal; Natale; Nowell

NORMAN, (Old English) Man from the north.

OLIVER, (Old French) Olive tree or branch.
Olivero; Olivier; Olliver; Oliveros; Ullivieri

OSCAR, (Old English) Divine spear.
Oskar; Oscaro; Osgar; Oskaras

PATRICK, (Latin) Small.
*Patricio; Patrizio; Patrizius; Padriac; Padraig;
Patric; Pavlos; Paultje; Pavel; Pouw*

PAUL, (Latin) Small.
*Paolo; Pablo; Paulino; Paulinus; Pol; Poul;
Pavelik; Pav; Paultje; Pavel; Pouw*

PETER, (Greek from Aramaic) Rock-like.
*Pedro; Pierre; Piers; Pies; Pieter; Pietro; Pijns;
Peader; Peder; Per; Perry; Petroc*

PHILIP, (Greek) Lover of horses.
*Phillip; Filippo; Filypas; Philipp; Phillipe; Piripi;
Filep; Filypas*

PREMYSL, (Bohemian) After the kings of
Bohemia.

RALPH, (Old Norse) Wolf Council.
Raul; Rahul; Rolf; Raoul; Rolph

RAYMOND, (Germanic) Mighty protector.
Raimondo; Raimund; Ramon; Rajmund

REINALDO, (Old English) Power and might.
*Reginald; Reggio; Reinald; Reinhold; Reinis;
Reinoldos; Rinaldo*

RENE, (Latin) Born again.
Renato; Renatus

REX, (Latin) King.

RHYS, (Welsh) Adour.
Reece; Rhett; Rees

RICHARD, (Old English) Hard ruler.
Ricardo; Rico; Ricard; Riik; Richie; Ricky

ROBERT, (Teutonic Germanic) Bright fame.
*Roberto; Robart; Robin; Robertino; Bob; Bobby;
Hrodert*

RODERIGO, (Teutonic) Famous ruler.
Roderick; Rodrigo; Rurik; Ruy; Rodrique

RODNEY, (English) A place name in
England.

ROGER, (Old English from Teutonic)
Famous spear.
*Ruggiero; Rogero; Rogier; Rutger; Hroger; Rogerio;
Rudiger; Rutger; Rutgert; Rodger; Rydygier*

ROLAND, (Teutonic) Famous land.
Rollo; Rowland; Orlando; Rolando

ROMANO, (Latin) From Rome.
Romanus; Roman; Romeo; Romulus

RONALD, (Germanic) Power.
Ronaldo; Reynald; Ranald; Reynaldo

RORY, (Irish) Red.

ROSS, (Gaelic) Promontory or isthmus.

ROWAN, ROHAN, (Old Norse/Saxon) Rowan or mountain ash tree.

ROY, (Celtic) Red or (French) King.

RUDOLPH, (Germanic) Famous wolf.
Rudolf; Ridolfo; Rodolf; Rudi; Hrudolf

RUPERT, (Germanic) Bright fame.
Ruperto; Ruberto; Rupprecht

RUSSELL, (Old French) Red hair or face.

RYAN, (Irish) Little king.

SALID, (Arabic) Lucky.

SALVATORE, (Italian) Saved.
Salvator; Salvador; Salvinus

SAMUEL, (Hebrew) Asked of God.
Sam; Samel; Sameli; Samolio; Samuil; Samuls; Schmul; Zamuels; Samueli

SCOTT, SCOT, A man from Scotland.

SEAMUS, SHAMUS, (Irish) Supplanter.

SEAN, (Irish form of John) Jehovah has favoured.
Shaun; Shawn

SEBASTIAN, (Latin) Man from Sebastia.
Sébastien; Sebaste; Sebastiano; Sebastyan; Sebastao; Sebastyen

SEID, (Arabic) Prince.
Sayid; Seyid

SIDNEY, SYDNEY, (English) Follower of St. Denis.

SIGFRID, (Teutonic) Victorious peace.
Siegfrid; Siegfried; Siffredo; Sigvard; Zygfryd

SIMON, (Hebrew) Harkening or listening.
Simeon; Simanao; Semein; Simone; Ssemar; Symon; Szymon

SOLOMON, (Hebrew) Worshipper of Shalman or little man of peace.
Salomo; Salomon; Salomone; Sulaiman; Zalman; Zelman; Salemonas

SPIRO, (Greek) Follower of St. Spiridion.
Spiridion; Spyridione

STANISLAUS, (Slavonic) Camp glory.
Stachis; Stanislas; Stanislavas; Stanislaw; Stanko; Stanislao; Stanislau

STANLEY, (Old English) Stony field.

STEPHEN, (Greek) Crown.
Steven; Stephan; Stepan; Stefan; Stefano; Stenka; Stavros; Stravopoulos; Stephanos; Stepko; Szczepan; Esteban; Estevan; Tepene

STUART, STEWART, (Old English) Steward of the household.

TAM, (Vietnamese) Heart.

TARIQ, TARIK, (Arabic) The night comer.

TERENCE, (Latin) Tender.
Terry; Thierry; Terencio; Terenz; Terrance

THEODORE, (Greek) God's gift.
Theo; Fedor; Feodor; Teodor; Teodorico; Teodoro; Todor

THOMAS, (Aramaic) Twin.
Tom; Dummas; Tamas; Tomasz; Tomaz; Tomasino; Tamassa; Tuomas; Toma; Tamati; Tomas; Didymus

TIMOTHY, (Greek) Honoured by God.
Timo; Timofee; Timotao; Timothée; Tymoteusz

TOBY, (Hebrew) Jehovah is good.
Tobias; Tobej; Tobies; Tobija; Tobit; Tobysas

TODD, (English from Norse) Bush or bushy-tailed fox.

TRAN, (Vietnamese) Old family name.

TRENT, (English) After the river.

TRISTAN, (Celtic) Tumult or din or sadness.
Tristram; Trystan

TROY, (Irish) Descendant of a foot soldier or from Troyes.

TYLER, (Old English) A tile maker.

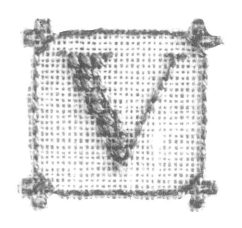

UMBERTO, (Teutonic) Big and bright.
Humbert; Humberto

VALENTINO, (Latin) Strong and healthy.
Valentine; Valentijn; Valentin; Valenty; Walenty

VAN, (Dutch) From or diminutive of Evan or Vanya.

VICTOR, (Latin) Conqueror.
Viktor; Vittorio; Wiktor

VINCENT, (Latin) Conquering.
Vincents; Vicente; Vikenty; Vincenzio; Vincens; Vincentz; Wincenty; Vincendo; Vincencio; Vincene

VLADIMIR, (Slavonic) Ruling power.
Vlad; Vladis; Vladislav; Vladislau; Valdemar; Waldemar; Wlodzimierz

WADE, (Old English) One who goes or wades.

WADUD, (Arabic) Loving.

WAJID, (Arabic) Finder.

WALLACE, WALLIS, (Scots) Strathclyde Welshman.

WALTER, (Teutonic) Ruler of folk.
Walther; Valter; Gualterius; Gualtier; Gualterio; Waltier

WARREN, (Germanic) Protector.

WARWICK, WARRICK, (Old English) Dairy farm at the weir.

WAYNE, (Old English) Waggoner.

WENCESLAS, (Slavonic) Crown of glory.
Vaclav; Venceslav; Waclaw; Wenzel; Vaacslav

WESLEY, (Old English) The west meadow.

WILFRED, (Old English) Will for peace.
Wilfrid; Wilfried

WILLIAM, (Germanic) Will and resolve helmut.
Bill; Billy; Liam; Wilhelm; Wille; Willem; Guillaume; Guglielmo; Guilhermo; Wilmer; Wimpje; Wiremu; Gwylym

WU, (Chinese) A province of China.

YURI, (Russian) Farmer.

ZACHARY, (Hebrew) Jehovah has remembered.
Zac; Zak; Zacharjasz; Zakariya; Zacharias; Zacharie; Zacharyasz; Zechariah; Zako

ZOLTAN, (Arabic) Sultan, ruler.

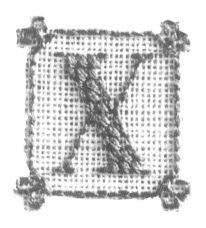

XAVIER, (Arabic) Brilliant.
Javier; Zaviero; Xavery; Savero

YOUR OWN GRAPH PAPER

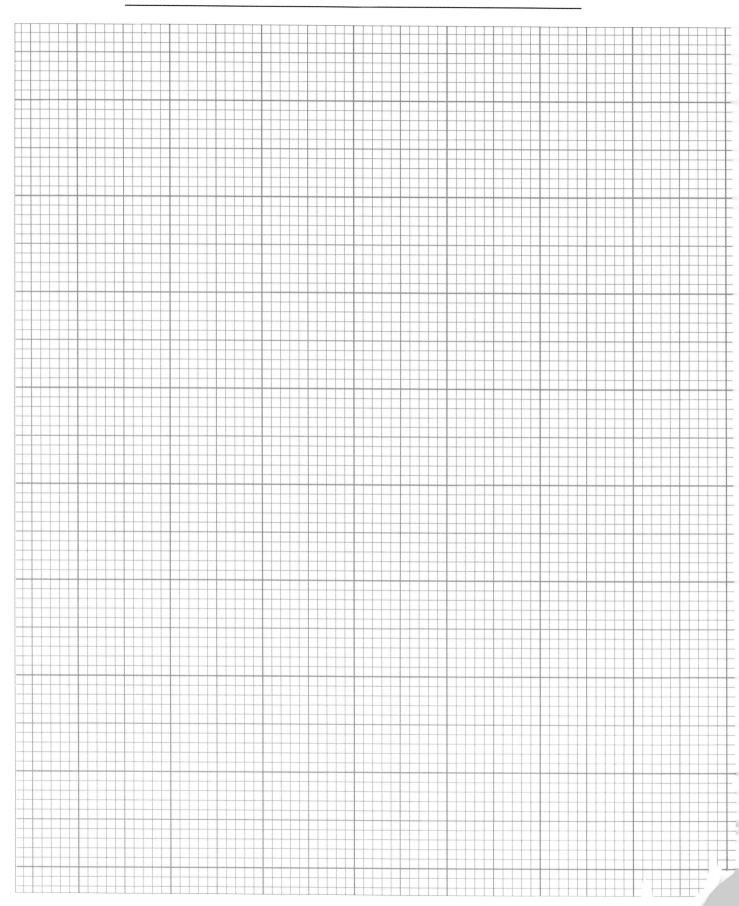

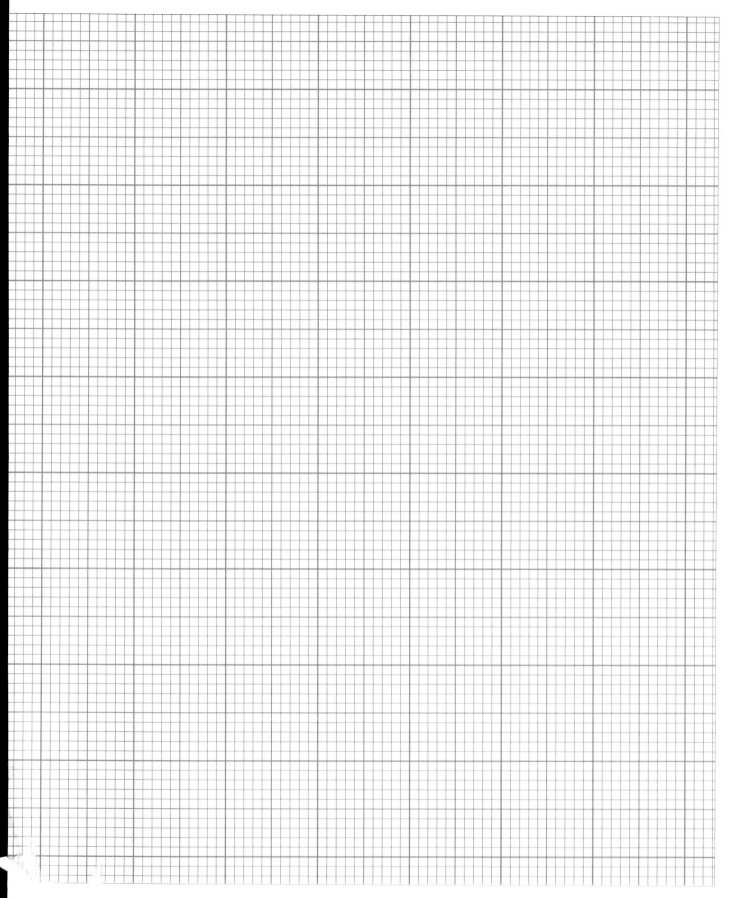

YOUR OWN GRAPH PAPER

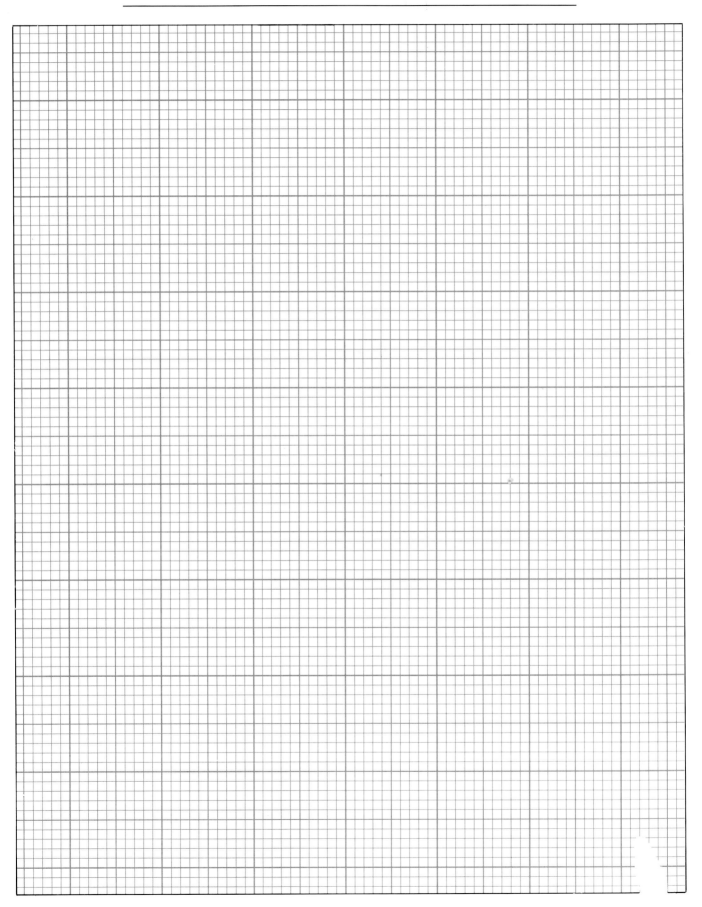

STOCKISTS

DMC Needlecraft
51-55 Carrington Road
Marrickville NSW 2204
Tel: (02) 559 3088

Michele Shennen's Garden Centre
185 High Street
Willoughby NSW 2068
Tel: (02) 958 6631

Sweet Violets
313 Pacific Highway
Lindfield NSW 2070
Tel: (02) 416 2572

Woodbridge
140 Edgecliff Road
Woollahra NSW 2025
Tel: (02) 387 2301

The assistance of DMC Needlecraft who provided the embroidery threads, evenweave fabrics and the bib is gratefully acknowledged.

CREATE YOUR OWN CRAFT COLLECTION WITH THE

BAY BOOKS TREASURY OF CRAFT

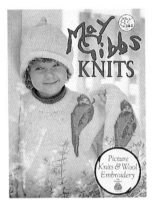    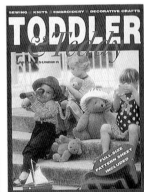

 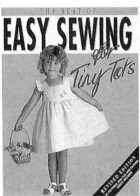  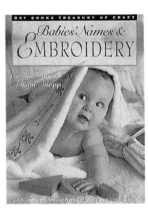 

If these titles are not available from your regular stockists, please write to the HarperCollins Sales Office in your State:

VICTORIA
22-24 JOSEPH ST
NORTH BLACKBURN
VIC 3130
TEL: (03) 895 8100
FAX: (03) 895 8199

NEW SOUTH WALES
25 RYDE RD
PYMBLE NSW 2073
TEL: (02) 952 5000
FAX: (02) 952 5777

QUEENSLAND
643 KESSELS ROAD
UPPER MOUNT GRAVATT
QLD 4122
TEL: (07) 849 7855
FAX:(07) 349 8286

SOUTH AUSTRALIA
UNIT 1 , 1-7 UNION STREET
STEPNEY SA 5069
TEL: (08) 363 0122
FAX:(08) 363 1653

WESTERN AUSTRALIA
SUITE 2 , 25 BELGRAVIA STREET
BELMONT WA 6104
TEL: (09) 479 4988
FAX: (09) 478 3248